Bake It Better

WITH QUAKER® OATS

CREDITS

Project Manager: Karen Doherty

Marketing Assistant: Lilly Yu

Recipe Development: The Quaker Kitchens
Mary Mulhall, Director
Karen Doherty, Manager

Photographers: Jim Wheeler, Kathy Sanders,
Russ Olsson, Deborah VanKirk

Food Stylists: Mary-Helen Steindler, Judy Vance,
Gail O'Donnell, Lois Hlavac

Prop Stylists: Nancy Wall Hopkins, Wendy Marx,
Marla Goldberg, Hilary Ashlund

Copy: McDowell & Piasecki Food
Communications, Inc.

NUTRITION INFORMATION

Nutrition information is provided for each of the recipes to help
with menu planning. This information is based on a nutrition analysis
of all ingredients, excluding optional ingredients. When an ingredient
choice is given, the analysis is based on the first ingredient listed.

 This symbol identifies those recipes or recipe variations
that contain 30 percent or fewer calories from fat.

 This symbol identifies those recipes that have been winners
in past Quaker Oatmeal Recipe Contests.

Cover photo: Chocolate Raspberry Streusel Squares (see page 19)
© 1995, The Quaker Oats Company
Published by Meredith Custom Publishing, 1995
Printed in Hong Kong

Bake It Better

WITH QUAKER® OATS

*Harvest Fruit Bars
(see page 25)*

*Banana Split Sundae
Cookies (see page 89)*

Cookies, Cookies, Cookies!

These oatmeal cookies are simply irresistible. Chock-full of chocolate, chewy fruit and crunchy nuts, flavored with vanilla and spice, chewy and crisp, plain and fancy, they are the Quaker Kitchens' best-loved and "most requested" recipes.

VANISHING OATMEAL RAISIN COOKIES

Crunchy, chewy, spicy…the ultimate oatmeal raisin cookie.

1 cup (2 sticks) margarine or butter, softened
1 cup firmly packed brown sugar
½ cup granulated sugar
2 eggs
1 teaspoon vanilla
1½ cups all-purpose flour
1 teaspoon baking soda
1 teaspoon ground cinnamon
½ teaspoon salt (optional)
3 cups QUAKER Oats (quick or old fashioned, uncooked)
1 cup raisins

Heat oven to 350°F. Beat together margarine and sugars until creamy. Add eggs and vanilla; beat well. Add combined flour, baking soda, cinnamon and salt; mix well. Stir in oats and raisins; mix well. Drop by rounded tablespoonfuls onto ungreased cookie sheet. Bake 10 to 12 minutes or until light golden brown. Cool 1 minute on cookie sheet; remove to wire rack. Cool completely. Store in tightly covered container.
ABOUT 4 DOZEN

VARIATIONS:
Ice Cream Sandwich Cookies
Spread softened ice cream on bottom side of one cookie; top with second cookie. Wrap airtight; freeze.

Chocolate-Dipped Cookies
Place 2 cups (12 ounces) semisweet chocolate pieces in dry 1-quart glass measuring cup or microwaveable bowl. Microwave at HIGH 1 to 2 minutes, stirring every 30 seconds, until smooth. Or, place in top part of double boiler over hot (not boiling) water; stir occasionally until smooth. Dip half of cookie in chocolate; gently shake to remove excess. Sprinkle with finely chopped nuts, if desired. Place on waxed paper until set. If chocolate thickens, microwave at 30-second intervals or set over hot water again until fluid.

Nutrition Information: 1 cookie
Calories 100, Fat 4g, Sodium 75mg

*Cocoa and chunks of chocolate make
these the most chocolatey oatmeal cookies around.*

1 cup (2 sticks) margarine or butter, softened
1 cup firmly packed brown sugar
½ cup granulated sugar
2 eggs
2 tablespoons water
1 teaspoon vanilla
4 cups QUAKER Oats (quick or old fashioned, uncooked)
1 cup all-purpose flour
2 tablespoons unsweetened cocoa powder
½ teaspoon baking soda
½ teaspoon salt (optional)
1 cup (6 ounces) semisweet chocolate pieces
Two 1.5-ounce milk chocolate bars, finely chopped

Heat oven to 350°F. Beat together margarine and sugars until creamy. Add eggs, water and vanilla; beat well. Add combined oats, flour, cocoa powder, baking soda and salt; mix well. Stir in chocolate pieces and chopped chocolate. Drop by rounded tablespoonfuls onto ungreased cookie sheet. Bake 12 to 14 minutes or until cookies are set. (Do not overbake.) Cool 1 minute on cookie sheet; remove to wire rack. Cool completely. Store in tightly covered container.
ABOUT 3½ DOZEN

Nutrition Information: 1 cookie
Calories 140, Fat 7g, Sodium 65mg

Perfect Drop Cookies

• Use the correct size cookie sheets.

• Preheat oven 10 to 15 minutes *before* baking.

• Once dry ingredients are added, don't beat vigorously or overmix.

• Use two spoons or a spoon and small spatula to scoop and push dough onto cookie sheet in evenly spaced mounds.

• Test for doneness after the *minimum* baking time.

• Cool cookie sheets completely between batches.

Bake It Better Tip

Bright, shiny cookie sheets prevent cookies from becoming too brown on the bottoms. Cookie sheets without rims help cookies brown more evenly.

QUAKER'S CHEWY CHOC-OAT-CHIP COOKIES

Chock-full of chocolate chips and nuts, they're quite simply the best chocolate chip cookies in town.

1	cup (2 sticks) margarine or butter, softened
1¼	cups firmly packed brown sugar
½	cup granulated sugar
2	eggs
2	tablespoons milk
2	teaspoons vanilla
1¾	cups all-purpose flour
1	teaspoon baking soda
½	teaspoon salt (optional)
2½	cups QUAKER Oats (quick or old fashioned, uncooked)
One	12-ounce package (2 cups) semisweet chocolate pieces
1	cup coarsely chopped nuts (optional)

Heat oven to 375°F. Beat together margarine and sugars until creamy. Add eggs, milk and vanilla; beat well. Add combined flour, baking soda and salt; mix well. Stir in oats, chocolate morsels and nuts; mix well. Drop by rounded tablespoonfuls onto ungreased cookie sheet.* Bake 9 to 10 minutes for a chewy cookie or 12 to 13 minutes for a crisp cookie. Cool 1 minute on cookie sheet; remove to wire rack. Cool completely. Store in tightly covered container.
ABOUT 5 DOZEN

For bar cookies: Press dough onto bottom of ungreased 13x9-inch baking pan. Bake 30 to 35 minutes or until light golden brown. Cool completely; cut into bars. Store tightly covered.
36 BARS

VARIATIONS:

Raisin Spice Oatmeal Cookies Prepare cookies as recipe directs, adding 1 teaspoon ground cinnamon and ¼ teaspoon ground nutmeg to dry ingredients. Substitute 1 cup raisins for chocolate pieces.

Signature Oatmeal Cookies Prepare cookies as recipe directs except substitute 1 cup (any combination of) raisins, diced dried mixed fruit, crushed toffee pieces or candy-coated chocolate pieces for 1 cup chocolate pieces.

Nutrition Information: 1 cookie
Calories 110, Fat 5g, Sodium 50mg

This Quaker classic began appearing on the package in the '80s and remains a "most requested" recipe.

1¼ cups (2½ sticks) margarine or butter, softened
¾ cup firmly packed brown sugar
½ cup granulated sugar
1 egg
1 teaspoon vanilla
1½ cups all-purpose flour
1 teaspoon baking soda
½ teaspoon salt (optional)
1 teaspoon ground cinnamon
¼ teaspoon ground nutmeg
3 cups QUAKER Oats (quick or old fashioned, uncooked)

Heat oven to 375°F. Beat together margarine and sugars until creamy. Add egg and vanilla; beat well. Add combined flour, baking soda, salt and spices; mix well. Stir in oats; mix well. Drop by rounded tablespoonfuls onto ungreased cookie sheet.* Bake 8 to 9 minutes for a chewy cookie or 10 to 11 minutes for a crisp cookie. Cool 1 minute on cookie sheet; remove to wire rack. Cool completely. Store in tightly covered container.
ABOUT 4½ DOZEN

For bar cookies: Press dough onto bottom of ungreased 13x9-inch baking pan. Bake 25 to 30 minutes or until light golden brown. Cool completely; cut into bars. Store tightly covered.
48 BARS

VARIATIONS:
• Stir in 1 cup raisins or chopped nuts.
• Stir in 1 cup semisweet chocolate, butterscotch or peanut butter flavored pieces; omit spices.

Nutrition Information: 1 cookie
Calories 90, Fat 5g, Sodium 70mg

Ingredients

In most recipes, either quick or old fashioned Quaker oats may be used. Old fashioned oats add more texture because the oats are left whole. Instant oatmeal is not recommended for baking.

Enjoy these crisp, delicate cookies with a glass of iced tea.

2 cups (4 sticks) margarine or butter, softened
1 cup sugar
1 tablespoon grated lemon peel
1 teaspoon vanilla
3 cups QUAKER Oats (quick or old fashioned, uncooked)
2 cups all-purpose flour
Powdered sugar (optional)

Beat together margarine, sugar, lemon peel and vanilla until creamy. Add oats and flour; mix well. Cover; chill about 30 minutes.

Heat oven to 350°F. Shape dough into 1-inch balls. Place 3 inches apart on ungreased cookie sheet. Flatten with bottom of glass dipped in granulated sugar. Bake 12 to 15 minutes or until edges are light golden brown. Cool 1 minute on cookie sheet; remove to wire rack. Cool completely. Sprinkle with powdered sugar, if desired. Store in tightly covered container. ABOUT 4½ DOZEN

Nutrition Information: 1 cookie
Calories 110, Fat 7g, Sodium 80mg

See photo page 16.

Ingredients

Either margarine or butter can be used to make the cookies in this book. Butter imparts a delicate flavor and a tender or crisp texture, depending upon the cookie. Cookies made with margarine have a similar texture and appearance but don't have a buttery flavor. Tub, soft, whipped and reduced-fat or reduced-calorie spreads should not be used. The added water and air in these products can cause cookies to be thin, flat and tough.

CHOCOLATE BROWNIE OATMEAL COOKIES

These fudgy drops have chewy, brownie-like centers
and plenty of crunchy nuts.

2 cups (12 ounces) semisweet chocolate pieces, melted*
One 8-ounce package cream cheese, softened
½ cup (1 stick) margarine or butter, softened
1 cup firmly packed brown sugar
½ cup granulated sugar
2 eggs
½ teaspoon vanilla
1½ cups all-purpose flour
1½ teaspoons baking soda
3 cups QUAKER Oats (quick or old fashioned, uncooked)
1 cup chopped nuts
Powdered sugar (optional)

Beat together cream cheese, margarine and sugars until creamy. Add eggs and vanilla; beat well. Add melted chocolate; mix well. Add combined flour and baking soda; mix well. Stir in oats and nuts; mix well. Cover; chill at least 1 hour.

Heat oven to 350°F. Shape dough into 1-inch balls. Place 3 inches apart on ungreased cookie sheet. Bake 8 to 10 minutes or until cookies are almost set. (Centers should still be moist. Do not overbake.) Cool 1 minute on cookie sheet; remove to wire rack. Cool completely. Sprinkle with powdered sugar, if desired. Store in tightly covered container.
ABOUT 6 DOZEN

*To melt chocolate: See Technique below.

Nutrition Information: 1 cookie
Calories 95, Fat 5g, Sodium 50mg

Technique — Melting Chocolate

Chocolate must be melted over very low heat and stirred constantly to prevent scorching. Be sure pan and utensils are dry; moisture can cause chocolate to become thick and grainy. If chocolate is in squares or bars, chop or break into uniform-size pieces. To microwave, place chocolate in microwaveable bowl or dry glass measuring cup. Microwave at HIGH 1 to 2 minutes, stirring every 30 seconds, until smooth. Or, place chocolate in the top part of double boiler over hot (not boiling) water. Stir occasionally until smooth.

Macadamia nuts and white and milk chocolate-striped candies add a contemporary twist to this cookie jar classic.

1 cup (2 sticks) margarine or butter, softened
1 cup firmly packed brown sugar
2 egg yolks
2 egg whites
1 teaspoon vanilla
2 cups QUAKER Oats (quick or old fashioned, uncooked)
1⅔ cups ground macadamia nuts or pecans, divided
1¼ cups all-purpose flour
48 foil-wrapped milk chocolate candies or white and chocolate-striped candies, unwrapped

Heat oven to 350°F. Lightly grease cookie sheet. Beat together margarine and sugar until creamy. Add egg yolks and vanilla; beat well.

Add combined oats, flour and ⅔ cup nuts; mix well. In small bowl, beat egg whites with fork until frothy. Shape dough into 1-inch balls. Dip in egg whites; press one side into remaining nuts. Place nut side up 1 inch apart on prepared cookie sheet; press thumb deeply in center of each. Bake 8 minutes; remove from oven. Place one chocolate piece in each center. Return to oven; continue baking 5 to 7 minutes or until cookies are lightly browned. Remove to wire rack; cool completely. Store in tightly covered container.
ABOUT 4 DOZEN

Nutrition Information: 1 cookie
Calories 130, Fat 8g, Sodium 50mg

Bake It Better Tip

For easier mixing, let butter or margarine stand at room temperature to soften. To soften in the microwave oven, microwave one stick on the lowest power setting, checking every 10 seconds. If the butter or margarine becomes too soft or begins to melt, don't use it for baking cookies as doing so will change a cookie's texture.

PEANUTTY CRISSCROSSES

*Keep plenty of these peanutty-good cookies on hand for
lunch bags and after-school snacks.*

¾ cup (1½ sticks) **margarine or butter,
softened**
1 cup **peanut butter**
1½ cups **firmly packed brown sugar**
⅓ cup **water**
1 **egg**
1 teaspoon **vanilla**
3 cups **QUAKER Oats (quick or
old fashioned, uncooked)**
1½ cups **all-purpose flour**
½ teaspoon **baking soda**
Granulated sugar

Beat together margarine, peanut butter and
sugar until creamy. Add water, egg and vanilla;
beat well. Add combined oats, flour and baking
soda; mix well. Cover; chill about 1 hour.

Heat oven to 350°F. Shape dough into 1-inch
balls. Place on ungreased cookie sheet; flatten
with tines of fork dipped in granulated sugar to
form crisscross pattern. Bake 9 to 10 minutes or
until edges are golden brown. Cool 2 minutes
on cookie sheet; remove to wire rack. Cool
completely. Store in tightly covered container.
ABOUT 7 DOZEN

Nutrition Information: 1 cookie
Calories 70, Fat 3g, Sodium 40mg

*Clockwise from top: Lemon Oat Lacies, Peanutty
Crisscrosses, Chocolate Raspberry Streusel Squares
and Ebony 'N' Ivory Brownies*

How To Store Cookies

• Cool cookies completely.

• Store crisp and soft cookies in separate
containers or the crisp cookies will soften;
store each kind of cookie separately so
flavors don't transfer.

• Separate very soft, fragile, frosted
or decorated cookies with a layer of
waxed paper.

• If cookies will be eaten in a day or two:
Store crisp cookies in a container with a
loose-fitting cover and soft cookies in a
container with a tight-fitting cover.
For longer storage, freeze in airtight
containers.

• Bar cookies may be stored in the
baking pan tightly covered.

Here's a black-tie brownie for special events.

1¼ cups (about 7 ounces) semisweet chocolate pieces, divided
⅔ cup (10 tablespoons plus 2 teaspoons) margarine or butter, softened
1 cup sugar
2 eggs
1 teaspoon vanilla
1¼ cups all-purpose flour
1 cup QUAKER Oats (quick or old fashioned, uncooked)
1 teaspoon baking powder
¼ teaspoon salt (optional)
One 4-ounce bar white chocolate, coarsely chopped, divided

Heat oven to 350°F. Lightly grease 13x9-inch baking pan. Melt 1 cup semisweet chocolate pieces according to directions at right; cool slightly. Beat together margarine, sugar, eggs and vanilla until smooth. Add melted chocolate; beat well. Add combined flour, oats, baking powder and salt; mix well. Stir in half of white chocolate. Spread batter into prepared pan. Bake 20 to 25 minutes or until brownies pull away from sides of pan. (Do not overbake.) Cool completely.

Melt remaining semisweet chocolate pieces and white chocolate separately, according to directions below. Drizzle over brownies. Let chocolate set before cutting into bars. Store tightly covered.
24 BARS

*To melt chocolate: Place in dry glass measuring cup or microwaveable bowl. Microwave at HIGH 1 to 2 minutes, stirring every 30 seconds, until smooth. Or place in top part of double boiler over hot (not boiling) water; stir occasionally until smooth.

Nutrition Information: 1 bar
Calories 190, Fat 10g, Sodium 90mg

See photo page 16.

Perfect Bar Cookies

• Use the correct size baking pan.

• Use fingers or the back of a large spoon to press stiff doughs into pan; use a spatula to spread batters evenly into pan. Use fingers to lightly pat oatmeal and crumb crusts onto bottom of pan.

• When testing bar cookies for doneness, your best guides are time and appearance. Use a timer and check after the *minimum* baking time.

• Cool bar cookies in their pan on a wire cooling rack.

*These elegant yet easy bars pair ribbons of chocolate and fruit
with a rich oatmeal cookie crust.*

1½ **cups all-purpose flour**
1½ **cups QUAKER Oats (quick or
     old fashioned, uncooked)**
 ½ **cup granulated sugar**
 ½ **cup firmly packed brown sugar**
 1 **teaspoon baking powder**
 ¼ **teaspoon salt (optional)**
 1 **cup (2 sticks) margarine or butter,
     chilled**
 1 **cup raspberry preserves or jam
     (about 10 ounces)**
 1 **cup (6 ounces) semisweet chocolate
     pieces**
 ¼ **cup chopped almonds**
 ½ **cup (3 ounces) semisweet chocolate
     pieces OR one 4-ounce bar white
     chocolate, chopped, melted*
     (optional)**

Heat oven to 375°F. Combine flour, oats, sugars, baking powder and salt. Cut in margarine until mixture is crumbly. Reserve 1 cup oat mixture for streusel; set aside. Press remaining oat

mixture onto bottom of ungreased 9-inch square baking pan. Bake 10 minutes. Spread preserves over crust; sprinkle evenly with chocolate pieces. Combine reserved oat mixture and almonds; sprinkle over chocolate pieces, patting gently. Bake 30 to 35 minutes or until golden brown. Cool completely. Drizzle with melted chocolate, if desired. Let chocolate set before cutting into squares. Store tightly covered.

36 SQUARES

*To melt chocolate: Place in dry glass measuring cup or microwaveable bowl. Microwave at HIGH 1 to 2 minutes, stirring every 30 seconds, until smooth. Or, place in top part of double boiler over hot (not boiling) water; stir occasionally until smooth.

Nutrition Information: 1 square
Calories 150, Fat 7g, Sodium 75mg

See front cover and photo page 16.

Ingredients

Better-quality white chocolate is available in blocks and bars. It is often located in the candy and confection aisle of the supermarket. Most of these products are a blend of cocoa butter, sugar, milk and flavorings. Don't confuse white chocolate with vanilla milk chips, vanilla-flavored candy coating or almond bark.

BERRY BERRY STREUSEL BARS

*A crisp crust and rich streusel topping surround
lots of sweet, juicy berries.*

1½ cups QUAKER Oats (quick or
     old fashioned, uncooked)
1¼ cups all-purpose flour
 ½ cup firmly packed brown sugar
 ¾ cup (1½ sticks) margarine or butter,
     melted
  1 cup fresh or frozen blueberries
 ⅓ cup raspberry or strawberry
     preserves
  1 teaspoon all-purpose flour
 ½ teaspoon grated lemon peel
     (optional)

Heat oven to 350°F. Combine oats, flour, sugar
and margarine; mix until crumbly. Reserve
1 cup oat mixture for streusel; set aside. Press
remaining oat mixture onto bottom of
ungreased 8- or 9-inch square baking pan.
Bake 13 to 15 minutes or until light golden
brown. Cool slightly. In medium bowl, combine
blueberries, preserves, flour and lemon peel;
mix gently. Spread over crust. Sprinkle with
reserved oat mixture, patting gently. Bake
20 to 22 minutes or until light golden brown.
Cool completely; cut into bars. Store tightly
covered.

16 BARS

Nutrition Information: 1 bar
Calories 190, Fat 9g, Sodium 110mg

Technique — Cutting Bar Cookies

Use a sharp knife to cut cookies into bars, squares, diamonds or other shapes as
desired. The following guidelines are approximate.

13 x 9-INCH BAKING PAN			8-INCH SQUARE BAKING PAN *		
Number of Rows	Size of Bar	Yield	Number of Rows	Size of Bar	Yield
6 x 6	2⅛ x 1½ in.	36	4 x 4	2 x 2 in.	16
8 x 5	1⅝ x 1¾ in.	40	4 x 5	2 x 1½ in.	20
8 x 6	1⅝ x 1½ in.	48	4 x 8	2 x 1 in.	32
6 x 9	2 x 1 in.	54	5 x 5	1½ x 1½ in.	25

*A 9-inch square pan will have the same yield, but cookies will be slightly larger.

PEANUT BUTTER 'N' FUDGE-FILLED BARS ★

This Grand Prize winner in the fourth annual Quaker Oatmeal Recipe Contest marries the flavors of three classic cookies – oatmeal, peanut butter and chocolate chip.

1 **cup (2 sticks) margarine or butter, softened**
2 **cups firmly packed brown sugar**
¼ **cup peanut butter**
2 **eggs**
2 **cups QUAKER Oats (quick or old fashioned, uncooked)**
2 **cups all-purpose flour**
1 **teaspoon baking soda**
¼ **teaspoon salt (optional)**
One **14-ounce can sweetened condensed milk (not evaporated milk)**
2 **cups (12 ounces) semisweet chocolate pieces**
2 **tablespoons peanut butter**
½ **cup chopped peanuts**

Heat oven to 350°F. Beat together margarine, sugar and ¼ cup peanut butter until creamy. Add eggs; beat well. Add combined oats, flour, baking soda and salt; mix well. Reserve 1 cup oat mixture for topping; set aside. Spread remaining oat mixture onto bottom of ungreased 13x9-inch baking pan. In medium saucepan, combine condensed milk, chocolate pieces and remaining 2 tablespoons peanut butter. Cook over low heat until chocolate is melted, stirring constantly. Remove from heat; stir in peanuts. Spread mixture evenly over crust. Drop reserved oat mixture by teaspoonfuls over chocolate mixture. Bake 25 to 30 minutes or until light golden brown. Cool completely; cut into bars. Store tightly covered.
32 BARS

Nutrition Information: 1 bar
Calories 280, Fat 14g, Sodium 140mg

Ingredients

Canned sweetened condensed milk is milk that has been cooked to reduce the water content and sweetened. Do not substitute evaporated milk for sweetened condensed milk.

The creative combination of fresh and dried fruits earned this layered bar cookie a first prize in the third annual Quaker Oatmeal Recipe Contest.

One 6-ounce package diced dried mixed fruit
1 cup diced banana (about 2 medium)
⅔ cup orange juice*
1½ teaspoons apple pie spice or ground cinnamon, divided
1 cup (2 sticks) margarine or butter, softened
1 cup firmly packed brown sugar
1¾ cups all-purpose flour
1½ cups QUAKER Oats (quick or old fashioned, uncooked)
½ cup chopped nuts

Heat oven to 375°F. In medium bowl, combine dried fruit, banana, orange juice and 1 teaspoon apple pie spice; set aside. Beat together margarine and sugar until creamy. Add combined flour, oats and remaining ½ teaspoon apple pie spice; mix well. Reserve ¾ cup oat mixture for topping; set aside. Press remaining oat mixture onto bottom of ungreased 13x9-inch baking pan. Bake 15 minutes. Remove from oven; spread fruit mixture evenly over crust to within ¼ inch of edges. Combine reserved oat mixture and nuts; sprinkle evenly over fruit, patting gently. Bake 16 to 20 minutes or until golden brown. Cool completely; cut into bars. Store loosely covered. 32 BARS

*If using old fashioned oats, decrease orange juice to ½ cup.

Nutrition Information: 1 bar
Calories 150, Fat 7g, Sodium 70mg

Bake It Better Tip

To measure oats, lightly spoon into dry nested measuring cup. Using a metal spatula or the straight edge of a table knife, level oats so they are even with the top of the cup.

OATMEAL CRUNCH TOFFEE BARS

These sweet treats look like a cookie but taste more like candy.

1 cup all-purpose flour
1 cup QUAKER Oats (quick or old fashioned, uncooked)
⅔ cup firmly packed brown sugar
½ teaspoon salt (optional)
⅔ cup (10 tablespoons plus 2 teaspoons) margarine or butter, melted
Five 1.4-ounce chocolate-covered toffee bars, chopped (about 1½ cups)
⅔ cup chopped nuts
½ cup butterscotch caramel fudge topping

Heat oven to 350°F. Lightly grease 9-inch square baking pan. Combine flour, oats, sugar and salt; mix well. Add margarine; mix until crumbly. Reserve ¾ cup oat mixture for topping; set aside. Press remaining oat mixture onto bottom of prepared pan. Bake 15 minutes. Sprinkle toffee bars and nuts evenly over crust; drizzle with caramel topping to within ½ inch of edges. Sprinkle with reserved oat mixture. Bake 22 to 25 minutes or until golden brown. Cool completely; cut into bars. Store tightly covered.

24 BARS

Nutrition Information: 1 bar
Calories 200, Fat 13g, Sodium 100mg

Bake It Better Tip

Bar cookies are easier to cut and remove from the baking pan when baked in a foil-lined pan. To line pan, cut foil large enough so that it will extend up all four sides. Press foil into pan, smoothing wrinkles and corners.

Grease foil only if recipe directs. To remove bars from pan, grasp extended edges of foil and lift. Transfer to cutting board and carefully peel off foil. Cut into bars.

CARAMEL OATMEAL CHEWIES

Caramel, chocolate and nuts equal irresistible.

1¾ cups QUAKER Oats (quick or old fashioned, uncooked)
1½ cups all-purpose flour
¾ cup firmly packed brown sugar
½ teaspoon baking soda
¼ teaspoon salt (optional)
¾ cup (1½ sticks) margarine or butter, melted
1 cup chopped nuts
1 cup (6 ounces) semisweet chocolate pieces
1 cup butterscotch caramel fudge topping
¼ cup all-purpose flour

Heat oven to 350°F. Lightly grease 13x9-inch baking pan. Combine oats, 1½ cups flour, sugar, baking soda and salt; mix well. Add margarine; mix until crumbly. Reserve 1 cup oat mixture for topping; set aside.

Press remaining oat mixture onto bottom of prepared pan. Bake 10 to 12 minutes or until light golden brown; cool 10 minutes. Top crust with nuts and chocolate pieces. Combine caramel topping and ¼ cup flour, mixing until smooth; drizzle over chocolate pieces to within ¼ inch of edges. Sprinkle with reserved oat mixture. Bake 18 to 22 minutes or until light golden brown. Cool completely; cut into bars. Store tightly covered.

32 BARS

Nutrition Information: 1 bar
Calories 200, Fat 9g, Sodium 105mg

Technique — Measuring

Before measuring sticky ingredients like ice cream topping, lightly coat inside of measuring cup with no-stick cooking spray. Topping will slip out, and measuring cup will be easier to clean.

Best Breads

Warm from the oven, a fresh-baked bread can add sparkle to the simplest breakfast. There are fruit-filled coffee cakes, more than a dozen different muffins, loaves for slicing and scrumptious scones to choose from. So, get baking!

BANANA-NANA PECAN BREAD

A packaged banana bread mix saves time, and the nutty oat topping makes this easy breakfast bread pretty as a picture.

1 **cup QUAKER Oats (quick or old fashioned, uncooked)**
½ **cup chopped pecans**
3 **tablespoons margarine or butter, melted**
2 **tablespoons firmly packed brown sugar**
One **14-ounce package banana bread quick bread mix**
1 **cup water**
½ **cup mashed ripe banana (about 1 large)**
2 **eggs, lightly beaten**
3 **tablespoons vegetable oil**

Heat oven to 375°F. Lightly grease and flour bottom only of 9x5-inch loaf pan. Combine oats, pecans, margarine and sugar; mix well. Reserve ½ cup oat mixture for topping; set aside. In large bowl, combine remaining oat mixture, quick bread mix, water, banana, eggs and oil. Mix just until dry ingredients are moistened. Pour into prepared pan. Sprinkle top of loaf with reserved oat mixture. Bake 50 to 55 minutes or until wooden pick inserted in center comes out clean. Cool 10 minutes in pan; remove to wire rack. Cool completely.
12 SERVINGS

Nutrition Information: ¹⁄₁₂ of recipe
Calories 270, Fat 12g, Sodium 250mg, Dietary Fiber 1g

See photo page 28.

Perfect Quick Bread Loaves

• Grease pan as directed in recipe. When pan sides are not greased, quick bread batters can climb higher and form a more rounded top.

• Measure accurately, and check the expiration date on the package to be sure baking powder and/or baking soda are fresh.

• Mix the dry ingredients with the liquid ingredients *only* until dry ingredients are moistened. Overmixing can make bread tough.

• Cool bread in pan on cooling rack 10 minutes. Loosen sides with metal spatula and turn out onto cooling rack.

• Don't worry if the baked loaf has a crack. A lengthwise crack is characteristic of many loaf-type quick breads.

You'll taste the tropics in every bite of this moist, fruit-filled bread.

BREAD
2½ cups all-purpose flour
1 cup QUAKER Oats (quick or old fashioned, uncooked)
½ cup sugar
2 teaspoons baking powder
½ teaspoon baking soda
½ teaspoon salt (optional)
¾ cup chopped dates or raisins
¾ cup orange juice
¾ cup mashed ripe banana (about 2 medium)
½ cup vegetable oil
2 eggs, lightly beaten
2 teaspoons grated orange peel
1 teaspoon vanilla

GLAZE (OPTIONAL)
½ cup powdered sugar
3 to 4 teaspoons orange juice
½ teaspoon grated orange peel

Heat oven to 350°F. For bread, lightly grease and flour bottom only of 9x5-inch loaf pan. Combine dry ingredients and dates; mix well. Add combined orange juice, banana, oil, eggs, orange peel and vanilla; mix just until dry ingredients are moistened. Pour into prepared pan. Bake 60 to 70 minutes or until wooden pick inserted in center comes out clean. Cool 10 minutes in pan; remove to wire rack. Cool completely. For glaze, combine all ingredients; mix until smooth. Drizzle over bread.

12 SERVINGS

Nutrition Information: 1/12 of recipe
Calories 300, Fat 11g, Sodium 120mg, Dietary Fiber 2g

Serving / Storage Tips

• Cool bread completely before slicing.

• Cut bread with a sharp, thin-bladed or serrated knife. Use a gentle sawing motion to prevent crumbling.

• If bread will be eaten in a day or two, wrap in foil or plastic wrap. For longer storage, wrap loaf securely in foil, or place in freezer bag. Seal, label and freeze for up to 6 months. Thaw at room temperature before serving.

Start the day with the goodness of oats baked in a muffin.
All nine delicious variations use the same basic batter.

STREUSEL

- ⅓ cup QUAKER Oats (quick or old fashioned, uncooked)
- ¼ cup all-purpose flour
- ¼ cup firmly packed brown sugar
- 3 tablespoons margarine or butter, chilled

MUFFINS

- 1½ cups all-purpose flour
- 1 cup QUAKER Oats (quick or old fashioned, uncooked)
- ½ cup sugar
- 1 tablespoon baking powder
- ¼ teaspoon salt (optional)
- 1 cup milk
- ¼ cup vegetable oil
- 1 egg, lightly beaten

Heat oven to 400°F. Line 12 medium muffin cups with paper baking cups, or lightly grease bottoms only. For streusel, combine dry ingredients; mix well. Cut in margarine until mixture is crumbly; set aside. For muffins, combine dry ingredients; mix well. Add combined milk, oil and egg; mix just until dry ingredients are moistened. Fill muffin cups ¾ full. Sprinkle streusel evenly over batter, patting gently. Bake 18 to 20 minutes or until golden brown. Let muffins stand a few minutes; remove from pan.

1 DOZEN

VARIATIONS:

Baker's D'Light Muffins
Substitute skim milk for milk and 2 egg whites for 1 whole egg. Omit streusel; sprinkle filled muffin cups evenly with ⅓ cup oats. ♥

Chocolate Surprise Muffins
Increase sugar to ⅔ cup and add ¼ cup unsweetened cocoa powder to dry ingredients. Add 1 teaspoon almond extract to liquid ingredients. Fill muffin cups ½ full. Spoon 1 teaspoon cherry or raspberry preserves in center of each muffin; top with remaining batter. Omit streusel; sprinkle tops of cooled muffins with powdered sugar, if desired. ♥

Star-Spangled Muffins
Add 1 teaspoon vanilla to liquid ingredients. Gently stir ½ cup *each* fresh or frozen blueberries and sliced strawberries into batter. Omit streusel. Sprinkle batter evenly with *Cinnamon-Sugar:* Mix together 1 tablespoon sugar and ¼ teaspoon ground cinnamon. ♥

Cranberry Orange Muffins
Add 1 cup coarsely chopped fresh or frozen cranberries and ½ cup chopped nuts to dry ingredients. Omit streusel. Drizzle *Citrus Glaze* over slightly cooled muffins: Mix together ¾ cup powdered sugar, 4 to 5 teaspoons orange juice and 1 teaspoon grated orange peel until smooth.

Whole Grain Raisin Muffins
Decrease flour to 1 cup. Add ¼ cup wheat germ and ½ teaspoon ground cinnamon to dry ingredients. Stir in ½ cup raisins with liquid ingredients. Omit streusel.♥

Banana Orange Muffins
Add 1 teaspoon ground cinnamon to dry ingredients. Substitute ¾ cup orange juice for milk and stir in 1 cup mashed ripe banana with liquid ingredients. Omit streusel. Drizzle *Citrus Glaze* over slightly cooled muffins: Mix together ¾ cup powdered sugar, 4 to 5 teaspoons orange juice and 1 teaspoon grated orange peel until smooth.♥

Peanut Butter 'N' Jelly Muffins
Add ¾ cup peanut butter to liquid ingredients. Fill muffin cups ½ full. Spoon 1 teaspoon any flavor jelly or fruit preserves in center of each muffin; top with remaining batter. Omit streusel.

Harvest Apple Muffins
Add 1 teaspoon ground cinnamon and ⅛ teaspoon ground nutmeg to dry ingredients. Substitute apple juice for milk and stir 1 cup chopped apple into batter.

Carrot Spice Muffins
Add 1 teaspoon ground cinnamon to dry ingredients. Stir in 1 cup shredded carrots and ½ cup raisins with liquid ingredients. Omit streusel. Spread tops of baked, cooled muffins with *Cream Cheese Frosting:* Mix together one 3-ounce package cream cheese, 2½ cups powdered sugar and 1 tablespoon milk until smooth.

Clockwise from bottom: Quaker's Best Oatmeal Muffin, Star-Spangled Muffin, Chocolate Surprise Muffin and Cranberry Orange Muffin

Nutrition Information: 1 Quaker's Best Oatmeal Muffin
Calories 240, Fat 9g, Sodium 170mg, Dietary Fiber 1g

Homemade carrot cake inspired these moist and tender muffins.

MUFFINS

- 1½ cups all-purpose flour
- 1 cup QUAKER Oats (quick or old fashioned, uncooked)
- ½ cup firmly packed brown sugar
- 1 tablespoon baking powder
- ½ teaspoon baking soda
- ½ teaspoon salt (optional)
- 1 teaspoon ground cinnamon
- ⅓ cup raisins
- One 8-ounce can crushed pineapple in juice, undrained
- ½ cup shredded carrots
- ½ cup skim milk
- ⅓ cup vegetable oil
- 2 egg whites or 1 egg, lightly beaten

GLAZE (OPTIONAL)

- ⅓ cup powdered sugar
- 3 to 4 teaspoons skim milk

Heat oven to 400°F. Line 12 medium muffin cups with paper baking cups, or lightly grease bottoms only. Combine dry ingredients and raisins; mix well. Add combined pineapple including juice, carrots, milk, oil and egg whites; mix just until dry ingredients are moistened. Fill muffin cups almost full. Bake 20 to 22 minutes or until golden brown. Let muffins stand a few minutes; remove from pan. Cool 10 minutes. For glaze, combine powdered sugar and milk; mix until smooth. Drizzle evenly over muffins.

1 DOZEN

Nutrition Information: 1 muffin
Calories 200, Fat 7g, Sodium 190mg, Dietary Fiber 2g

Perfect Muffins

- Grease muffin cups as directed in recipe, or line with paper baking cups.

- Thoroughly combine dry ingredients in one bowl and liquid ingredients in a second bowl.

- Add liquid ingredients to dry ingredients all at once and stir with a large spoon *just* until dry ingredients are moistened — 15 to 20 light strokes. There should be some lumps.

- Immediately spoon batter into muffin cups, filling each cup between two-thirds and three-fourths full.

- Bake in a preheated, hot oven.

- Test for doneness by inserting a wooden pick into the center of one muffin. If pick comes out with a few moist crumbs clinging to it, the muffins are done.

- Cool a minute or two in the pan, then remove to keep muffins from becoming soggy.

PUMPKIN OAT STREUSEL MUFFINS

A crunchy streusel topping made with whole grain oats and brown sugar complements the pumpkin and spice.

STREUSEL

- ¼ cup QUAKER Oats (quick or old fashioned, uncooked)
- 1 tablespoon firmly packed brown sugar
- 1 tablespoon margarine or butter, melted
- ⅛ teaspoon pumpkin pie spice

MUFFINS

- 1½ cups all-purpose flour
- 1 cup QUAKER Oats (quick or old fashioned, uncooked)
- ¾ cup firmly packed brown sugar
- 1 tablespoon baking powder
- 1½ teaspoons pumpkin pie spice
- ½ teaspoon baking soda
- ½ teaspoon salt (optional)
- ½ cup chopped nuts (optional)
- 1 cup canned pumpkin
- ¾ cup milk
- ⅓ cup vegetable oil
- 1 egg, lightly beaten

Heat oven to 400°F. Line 12 medium muffin cups with paper baking cups, or lightly grease bottoms only. For streusel, combine all ingredients; mix well. Set aside. For muffins, combine dry ingredients and nuts; mix well. Add combined pumpkin, milk, oil and egg; mix just until dry ingredients are moistened. Fill muffin cups almost full. Sprinkle streusel evenly over batter, patting gently. Bake 22 to 25 minutes or until golden brown. Let muffins stand a few minutes; remove from pan.
1 DOZEN

Nutrition Information: 1 muffin

Calories 230, Fat 9g, Sodium 170mg, Dietary Fiber 2g

Maple-flavored syrup and sweet-tart apples are a winning combination.

MUFFINS

1⅓	cups all-purpose flour
1	cup QUAKER Oats (quick or old fashioned, uncooked)
½	cup granulated sugar
1	tablespoon baking powder
1½	teaspoons ground cinnamon
½	cup milk
⅓	cup (5 tablespoons plus 1 teaspoon) margarine or butter, melted
¼	cup maple-flavored syrup
2	egg whites or 1 egg, lightly beaten
1	cup chopped apple (about 1 medium)
	Pecan halves (optional)

GLAZE (OPTIONAL)

3	tablespoons powdered sugar
1	tablespoon maple-flavored syrup

Heat oven to 400°F. Line 12 medium muffin cups with paper baking cups, or lightly grease bottoms only.* For muffins, combine dry ingredients; mix well. Add combined milk, margarine, syrup and egg whites; mix just until dry ingredients are moistened. Gently stir in apple. Fill muffin cups almost full. Top each with pecan half, if desired. Bake 20 to 25 minutes or until golden brown. Let muffins stand a few minutes; remove from pan. Cool 10 minutes. For glaze, combine powdered sugar and syrup; mix until smooth. Drizzle over muffins.

1 DOZEN

*Or use 30 miniature muffin cups. Bake 10 to 12 minutes or until golden brown.

Nutrition Information: 1 muffin

Calories 200, Total Fat 6g, Saturated Fat 1g, Cholesterol 0mg, Sodium 190mg, Dietary Fiber 1g

Bake It Better Tip

In a hurry? Wash apples but don't peel. You'll be adding color and additional fiber, too.

To Freeze

All of the muffins in this book may be frozen. To freeze, wrap muffins securely in foil, or place in freezer bag. Seal, label and freeze for up to six months.

To Reheat

Place foil-wrapped muffins in 350°F oven, and heat 15 to 20 minutes. To reheat in microwave oven, place unwrapped muffin on napkin, microwave-safe paper towel or plate. Microwave at HIGH about 30 seconds for each muffin.

*This elegant but easy coffee cake won a second prize in the second annual
Quaker Oatmeal Recipe Contest.*

CAKE/CRUMB TOPPING

- 1½ cups all-purpose flour
- ¾ cup QUAKER Oats (quick or old fashioned, uncooked)
- ¾ cup granulated sugar
- 1 teaspoon ground cinnamon
- ½ teaspoon baking powder
- ½ teaspoon baking soda
- ½ teaspoon ground nutmeg
- ¼ teaspoon salt (optional)
- ½ cup (1 stick) margarine or butter, chilled
- ¼ cup low-fat ricotta cheese
- ¾ cup nonfat or light sour cream
- 2 egg whites, lightly beaten

FILLING

- 2 cups chopped apple (about 2 medium)
- ⅓ cup seedless raspberry jam
- 2 teaspoons all-purpose flour
  Powdered sugar

Heat oven to 350°F. Lightly grease 9-inch springform or round cake pan. For cake and topping, combine dry ingredients; mix well. Cut in margarine and ricotta cheese until mixture is crumbly. Reserve 1½ cups oat mixture for topping; set aside. Combine sour cream and egg whites; add to remaining oat mixture, mixing just until moistened. Spread batter over bottom and ½ inch up sides of prepared pan. For filling, combine apples, jam and flour; spoon over cake. Sprinkle reserved oat mixture over fruit. Bake 50 to 55 minutes or until golden brown. Sprinkle with powdered sugar. Serve warm.

12 SERVINGS

Nutrition Information: ¹⁄₁₂ of cake

Calories 250, Fat 9g, Sodium 170mg, Dietary Fiber 1g

Ingredients

Their tart flavor and firm texture make these apple varieties best for baking: Jonathan, McIntosh, Winesap, Granny Smith, Northern Spy, Greening and Rome Beauty. One medium apple equals about 1 cup sliced or chopped apple.

VERY BERRY BREAKFAST CAKE

*Make Sunday breakfast a family tradition and ease into the day
with a from-scratch, berry-filled coffee cake.*

STREUSEL
- ½ **cup QUAKER Oats (quick or old fashioned, uncooked)**
- ¼ **cup sugar**
- 3 **tablespoons margarine or butter, melted**
- ¼ **teaspoon ground cinnamon**

COFFEE CAKE
- ½ **cup (1 stick) margarine or butter, softened**
- 1 **cup sugar**
- 4 **egg whites or 2 eggs, lightly beaten**
- One **8-ounce carton light sour cream**
- 1 **teaspoon vanilla**
- 1½ **cups all-purpose flour**
- ¾ **cup QUAKER Oats (quick or old fashioned, uncooked)**
- 2 **teaspoons baking powder**
- ½ **teaspoon baking soda**
- ⅓ **cup raspberry preserves**
- ¾ **cup fresh or frozen blueberries**

Heat oven to 350°F. Lightly grease 9-inch square baking pan. For streusel, combine all ingredients; mix well. Set aside. For coffee cake, beat margarine and sugar until creamy. Add egg whites, sour cream and vanilla; beat well. Add combined flour, oats, baking powder and baking soda; mix just until dry ingredients are moistened. Spread into prepared pan. Spoon preserves over batter; swirl through batter with knife. Sprinkle blueberries evenly over batter. Sprinkle streusel over blueberries. Bake 50 to 55 minutes or until wooden pick inserted in center comes out clean. Serve warm. Store leftovers tightly covered.

12 SERVINGS

Nutrition Information: ¹/₁₂ of recipe
Calories 330, Fat 14g, Sodium 250mg, Dietary Fiber 2g

Ingredients

Berries are very perishable. Store in refrigerator until ready to use, then wash and pat dry. To freeze, arrange washed and dried berries in single layer in shallow pan and freeze until firm. Transfer frozen berries to freezer bag; label and freeze. Don't thaw berries before using.

SCOTTISH OAT SCONES

Similar to a biscuit, scones pair comfortably with a breakfast mug of java or an afternoon cup of tea.

1½ cups all-purpose flour
1 cup QUAKER Oats (quick or old fashioned, uncooked)
¼ cup sugar
1 tablespoon baking powder
¼ teaspoon salt (optional)
½ cup (1 stick) margarine or butter, chilled
½ cup currants
⅓ cup milk
1 egg, lightly beaten
1 tablespoon sugar
⅛ teaspoon ground cinnamon

Heat oven to 400°F. Lightly grease cookie sheet. Combine flour, oats, sugar, baking powder and salt; mix well. Cut in margarine with pastry blender or two knives until mixture resembles coarse crumbs. Stir in currants. Add combined milk and egg; mix with fork just until dry ingredients are moistened. Turn out onto lightly floured surface; knead gently 8 to 10 times. Roll or pat dough into 8-inch circle about ½ inch thick. Sprinkle with combined 1 tablespoon sugar and cinnamon. Cut into 10 wedges; place on prepared cookie sheet. Bake 12 to 15 minutes or until light golden brown. Serve warm.
10 SCONES

VARIATIONS:
Substitute raisins, diced dried mixed fruit, dried cherries, cranberries or blueberries for currants, if desired.

Nutrition Information: 1 scone
Calories 240, Fat 11g, Sodium 275mg, Dietary Fiber 2g

Technique — Cutting In

When making biscuits and scones as well as some cookies and cakes, the fat is distributed throughout the dry ingredients using a technique called "cutting in." Using a pastry blender, two knives in a scissors motion or your fingertips, work chilled margarine, butter or shortening into the combined dry ingredients until mixture resembles coarse crumbs.

Quick-rising yeast shortens the rising time for this classic oatmeal bread by almost half.

5¾ to 6¼ cups all-purpose flour
2½ cups QUAKER Oats (quick or
    old fashioned, uncooked)
¼ cup sugar
Two ¼-ounce packages quick-rising yeast
2½ teaspoons salt
1½ cups water
1¼ cups milk
¼ cup (½ stick) margarine or butter

In large mixing bowl, combine 3 cups flour, oats, sugar, yeast and salt; mix well. Heat water, milk and margarine until warm (120°F to 130°F). Add to flour mixture. Blend at low speed of electric mixer until moistened; beat 3 minutes at medium speed. By hand, gradually stir in enough remaining flour to make a firm dough.

Lightly grease large bowl. Turn dough out onto lightly floured surface. Knead 5 to 8 minutes or until smooth and elastic. Shape to form ball; place in prepared bowl, turning once. Cover; let rise in warm place 30 minutes or until double in size.

Grease two 8x4- or 9x5-inch loaf pans. Punch down dough. Cover; let rest 10 minutes. Divide dough in half. Shape to form 2 loaves; place in pans. Brush lightly with melted margarine; sprinkle with oats, if desired. Cover; let rise in warm place 10 to 15 minutes or until nearly double in size. Heat oven to 375°F. Bake 45 to 50 minutes or until dark golden brown. Remove from pans; cool on wire rack.
2 LOAVES

Nutrition Information: ¹⁄₁₆ of loaf
Calories 130, Total Fat 2g, Saturated Fat 0g, Cholesterol 0mg,
Sodium 210mg, Dietary Fiber 1g

Bake It Better Tip

To be sure dough has risen enough, lightly press two fingers about ½ inch into center of dough. If the indentations remain, the dough has risen sufficiently.

Technique — Kneading

Knead dough on lightly floured surface. 1. Place heels of both hands in center of dough; push dough forward as far as possible. 2. Fold dough in half. 3. Pick up folded dough and turn it a quarter turn. Then repeat steps 1, 2 and 3 until dough is smooth and elastic, about 5 minutes.

Irresistible Desserts

At the end of a meal,
or in the middle of
the day, dessert is
an indulgence that won't
break the budget.
From comforting fruit
cobblers and crisps,
to lusciously rich
cheesecake, there's a
dessert to satisfy every
sweet tooth.

*An early cook coined the name "cobbler" because the
biscuit topping resembles a cobbled street.*

Two 16-ounce cans pitted sour cherries*
¾ cup sugar
2 tablespoons cornstarch
⅛ teaspoon almond extract (optional)
**1 cup QUAKER Oats (quick or old
      fashioned, uncooked)**
1 cup all-purpose flour
¼ cup sugar
2 teaspoons baking powder
¼ teaspoon salt (optional)
**⅓ cup (5 tablespoons plus 1 teaspoon)
      margarine or butter, chilled**
**½ cup milk
      Whipped cream or ice cream
      (optional)**

Drain cherries, reserving 1 cup liquid. In
medium saucepan, combine ¾ cup sugar and
cornstarch; stir in reserved liquid. Bring to a
boil over medium high heat, stirring constantly
until thickened and clear. Reduce heat; boil
1 minute. Stir in cherries and almond extract.
Pour mixture into 10-inch round quiche dish
or 8-inch square glass baking dish.

Heat oven to 400°F. Combine oats, flour, ¼ cup
sugar, baking powder and salt; mix well. Cut in
margarine with pastry blender or two knives
until mixture resembles coarse crumbs. Add
milk; mix with fork just until dry ingredients
are moistened. Drop by rounded tablespoonfuls
over hot filling. Bake 25 to 30 minutes or until
topping is light golden brown. Serve warm with
whipped cream or ice cream, if desired.
9 SERVINGS

*NOTE: Two 20-ounce cans cherry pie filling may be
substituted for sour cherries. Omit sugar and cornstarch;
proceed as recipe directs.

Nutrition Information: ⅑ of recipe
Calories 280, Total Fat 8g, Saturated Fat 1g, Cholesterol 0mg, Sodium 200mg,
Dietary Fiber 1g

See photo page 44.

Bake It Better Tip

**The dough used to make a fruit cobbler is
really a sweetened baking powder biscuit.
As with biscuits, be sure not to overmix
dough or biscuits will be tough.**

A fruit-filled shortcake makes a dazzling finale for a special meal.

SHORTCAKE

- **1 cup QUAKER Oats (quick or old fashioned, uncooked)**
- **1 cup all-purpose flour**
- **¼ cup sugar**
- **1 tablespoon grated orange or lemon peel**
- **1 tablespoon baking powder**
- **½ teaspoon baking soda**
- **½ teaspoon salt (optional)**
- **¼ cup (½ stick) margarine or butter, chilled**
- **⅔ cup plain low-fat yogurt**

TOPPING

- **One 8-ounce carton plain low-fat yogurt**
- **1 cup sliced banana (about 1 large)**
- **½ cup fresh raspberries**
- **½ cup fresh blueberries**
- **Ground cinnamon**

Heat oven to 425°F. Lightly grease 8-inch round cake pan. Combine oats, flour, sugar, orange peel, baking powder, baking soda and salt; mix well. Cut in margarine with pastry blender or two knives until mixture resembles coarse crumbs. Add yogurt; mix with fork just until dry ingredients are moistened. Turn out onto lightly floured surface. Knead gently 8 to 10 times. Pat into prepared pan. Bake 15 to 20 minutes or until golden brown. Cool 5 minutes in pan. Remove to wire rack; cool slightly. To serve, cut shortcake into 8 wedges. Top with about 2 tablespoons yogurt and ¼ cup combined fruit mixture. Sprinkle with cinnamon.

8 SERVINGS

Nutrition Information: ⅛ of recipe

Calories 210, Total Fat 7g, Saturated Fat 1g, Cholesterol 0mg, Sodium 300mg, Dietary Fiber 2g

Serving Suggestion

Substitute lightly sweetened whipped cream for the yogurt topping. Split warm shortcake wedges in half horizontally, and layer with fruit and cream.

Traditional apple crisp is one of the Quaker Kitchens' "most requested" recipes.
Peaches and pears are equally delicious.

1 **cup QUAKER Oats (quick or old fashioned, uncooked)**
½ **cup coarsely chopped nuts (optional)**
¼ **cup firmly packed brown sugar**
¼ **cup (½ stick) margarine or butter, melted**
¼ **teaspoon ground cinnamon**
6 **cups peeled, thinly sliced apples, peaches or pears (about 6 to 8 medium)**
¼ **cup water**
¼ **cup firmly packed brown sugar**
2 **tablespoons all-purpose flour**
½ **teaspoon ground cinnamon**
Vanilla ice cream or whipped cream (optional)

Heat oven to 350°F. Combine oats, nuts, ¼ cup brown sugar, margarine and ¼ teaspoon cinnamon; mix well. Set aside. In large bowl, combine fruit and water. Add remaining brown sugar, flour and cinnamon, tossing to coat. Spoon into 8-inch square glass baking dish. Top with reserved oat mixture. Bake 30 to 35 minutes or until fruit is tender. Serve warm with ice cream or whipped cream, if desired.
9 SERVINGS

MICROWAVE DIRECTIONS:
Follow recipe as directed above except spoon fruit mixture into 8-inch square microwaveable dish; set aside oat mixture. Microwave at HIGH 6 minutes, stirring once. Top with reserved oat mixture. Microwave at HIGH 3 to 6 minutes or until fruit is tender.

Nutrition Information: ⅑ of recipe
Calories 200, Total Fat 6g, Saturated Fat 1g, Cholesterol 0mg
Sodium 65mg, Dietary Fiber 4g

Toppers for Crisps and Cobblers

- A scoop of ice cream or frozen yogurt
- Half and half or heavy cream
- Lightly sweetened whipped cream
- Vanilla or fruit-flavored yogurt
- Cheddar or colby cheese (especially good with apple and pear crisps and cobblers)
- Lightly sweetened ricotta cheese
- Custard sauce

Lazy Daisy Cake debuted in the 1950s and quickly became a popular family dessert. Now it's been updated to trim the fat and cholesterol but not the flavor of the moist spice cake and candy-like topping.

CAKE

- 1¼ cups boiling water
- 1 cup QUAKER Oats (quick or old fashioned, uncooked)
- ⅓ cup (5 tablespoons plus 1 teaspoon) margarine or butter, softened
- 1 cup granulated sugar
- 1 cup firmly packed brown sugar
- 2 egg whites or 1 egg
- 1 teaspoon vanilla
- 1¾ cups all-purpose flour
- 1 teaspoon baking soda
- 1 teaspoon ground cinnamon
- ¼ teaspoon ground nutmeg (optional)
- ¼ teaspoon salt (optional)

TOPPING

- ½ cup flaked coconut
- ½ cup firmly packed brown sugar
- ½ cup QUAKER Oats (quick or old fashioned, uncooked)
- 3 tablespoons skim milk
- 2 tablespoons margarine or butter, melted

Heat oven to 350°F. Lightly grease and flour 8- or 9-inch square baking pan. For cake, pour boiling water over oats; set aside. Beat margarine and sugars until creamy. Add egg whites and vanilla; beat well. Add oat mixture and combined dry ingredients; mix well. Pour batter into prepared pan. Bake 55 to 65 minutes (8x8-inch pan) or 50 to 60 minutes (9x9-inch pan) or until wooden pick inserted in center comes out clean.

For topping, combine all ingredients; mix well. Spread evenly over top of warm cake. Broil about 4 inches from heat 1 to 2 minutes or until topping is bubbly. Watch closely; topping burns easily. Cool cake in pan on wire rack. Store tightly covered.

12 SERVINGS

Nutrition Information: ¹⁄₁₂ of recipe

Calories 360, Total Fat 9g, Saturated Fat 2g, Cholesterol 0mg, Sodium 220mg, Dietary Fiber 2g

Ingredients

Most cake recipes today call for all-purpose flour. All-purpose flour can be bleached or unbleached. Although they can be used interchangeably, bleached flour produces a cake with a finer texture.

*Sliced bananas and Hawaiian macadamia nuts add a tropical twist
to pineapple upside-down cake.*

TOPPING

2	tablespoons margarine or butter
¼	cup chopped macadamia nuts or almonds
⅓	cup firmly packed brown sugar
One	8-ounce can pineapple tidbits, well drained
½	cup sliced banana (about 1 medium)

CAKE

½	cup (1 stick) margarine or butter, softened
1	cup granulated sugar
1	teaspoon vanilla
⅔	cup milk
4	egg whites or 2 eggs
1½	cups all-purpose flour
¾	cup QUAKER Oats (quick or old fashioned, uncooked)
1	tablespoon baking powder

Heat oven to 350°F. For topping, place margarine and nuts in 9-inch square baking pan; bake 5 to 7 minutes or until margarine is melted and nuts are lightly browned. Sprinkle brown sugar over nuts; top with fruit. Set aside.

For cake, beat together margarine, sugar and vanilla until creamy. Add milk and egg whites; beat well. Add combined flour, oats and baking powder; mix well. Spread evenly over fruit mixture. Bake 45 to 50 minutes or until wooden pick inserted in center comes out clean. Loosen edges of cake from pan; invert immediately onto serving platter. Serve warm.
12 SERVINGS

Nutrition Information: ¹⁄₁₂ of recipe
Calories 300, Fat 12g, Sodium 250mg, Dietary Fiber 1g

Perfect Cakes

• Unless recipe directs otherwise, grease and lightly flour pan(s).

• Have all ingredients at room temperature.

• Preheat oven at least 15 minutes *before* baking.

• Begin testing for doneness after the *minimum* baking time. If wooden pick inserted in center of cake comes out with a few moist crumbs clinging to it, the cake is done.

BANANA CRUNCH CAKE

You'll go bananas over this moist banana cake with a crunchy oat and nut topping.

STREUSEL
- ¼ **cup QUAKER Oats (quick or old fashioned, uncooked)**
- ¼ **cup all-purpose flour**
- ¼ **cup firmly packed brown sugar**
- 3 **tablespoons margarine or butter, chilled**
- ¼ **cup chopped nuts**

CAKE
- ½ **cup (1 stick) margarine or butter, softened**
- ⅔ **cup firmly packed brown sugar**
- 1 **cup mashed ripe banana (about 3 medium)**
- 2 **eggs**
- 1 **teaspoon vanilla**
- 1 **cup QUAKER Oats (quick or old fashioned, uncooked)**
- 1 **cup all-purpose flour**
- 1 **teaspoon baking soda**
- ½ **teaspoon salt (optional)**

Heat oven to 350°F. Lightly grease 8-inch square baking pan. For topping, combine oats, flour and sugar; mix well. Cut in margarine until mixture is crumbly. Stir in nuts; set aside.

For cake, beat together margarine and sugar until creamy; add banana, eggs and vanilla; beat well. Add combined oats, flour, baking soda and salt. Mix just until dry ingredients are moistened. Pour into prepared pan. Sprinkle streusel evenly over batter, patting gently. Bake 35 to 40 minutes or until wooden pick inserted in center comes out clean. Cool completely on wire rack. Store tightly covered.

9 SERVINGS

Nutrition Information: ⅑ of recipe
Calories 380, Fat 19g, Sodium 350mg, Dietary Fiber 2g

Ingredients

Really ripe bananas give baked products the most intense flavor. Look for bananas that are deep yellow and speckled with brown. Three medium bananas (about 1 pound) equal 1 cup mashed.

Technique: Scrape sides of mixing bowl frequently with rubber spatula.

53

CHOCOLATE CHIP CHEESECAKE

The oatmeal cookie crust sets this cheesecake apart from the competition.

CRUST

1½ **cups QUAKER Oats (quick or old fashioned, uncooked)**
½ **cup finely chopped nuts**
⅓ **cup firmly packed brown sugar**
⅓ **cup (5 tablespoons plus 1 teaspoon) margarine or butter, melted**

FILLING

Three **8-ounce packages cream cheese, softened**
1 **cup granulated sugar**
1½ **teaspoons vanilla**
3 **eggs**
⅓ **cup milk or strong coffee**
1 **cup mini semisweet chocolate pieces**
2 **teaspoons all-purpose flour**

Heat oven to 350°F. For crust, combine all ingredients; mix well. Press onto bottom and 1 inch up sides of 9-inch springform pan or bottom only of 13x9-inch baking pan. Bake 10 to 15 minutes or until golden brown. Cool completely.

For filling, beat together cream cheese, sugar and vanilla until smooth. Add eggs, one at a time, beating well after each. Gradually add milk; beat well. Reserve 1 tablespoon chocolate pieces. Combine remaining chocolate pieces with flour; stir into cream cheese mixture. Pour over crust. Sprinkle with reserved chocolate pieces. Bake 50 to 60 minutes (45 minutes for 13x9-inch pan) or until almost set. Cool completely. Loosen cheesecake from sides of pan; remove rim. Chill.

16 SERVINGS

Nutrition Information: 1/16 of recipe
Calories 370, Fat 25g, Sodium 190mg, Dietary Fiber 1g

Perfect Cheesecakes

• Let cream cheese stand at room temperature until softened. Cream cheese that is too cold will form small lumps in the batter.

• Use lightly buttered fingers or the back of a spoon to firmly press oat crust evenly in pan.

• Cool crust completely before adding filling.

• To test cheesecake for doneness, grasp sides of pan with oven mitts and *gently* move pan. *(Do not shake or cheesecake might crack.)* If very center of cheesecake jiggles, remove to wire cooling rack. During cooling, center will continue cooking and become firm.

• Cool cheesecake completely on wire rack. Loosen sides with spatula or knife, remove pan rim, cover and refrigerate.

*Frozen yogurt, fresh fruit and lite fudge topping are what make
this dessert deliciously guilt-free.*

CRUST

**1 cup QUAKER Oats (quick or
old fashioned, uncooked)**

½ cup all-purpose flour

**⅓ cup (5 tablespoons plus 1 teaspoon)
margarine or butter, melted**

¼ cup firmly packed brown sugar

FILLING/TOPPINGS

**One 1-quart carton vanilla nonfat
frozen yogurt**

**2 cups any combination fresh fruit
Lite hot fudge topping**

Heat oven to 350°F. Lightly grease 9-inch pie
plate. For crust, combine all ingredients; mix
well. Press mixture evenly onto bottom and
sides of prepared pie plate. Bake 18 to 20
minutes or until golden brown. Cool
completely.

Let yogurt stand at room temperature until
softened, about 20 minutes. Spoon into cooled
crust, spreading evenly. Cover loosely; freeze
about 5 hours or until firm. Remove pie from
freezer 10 to 15 minutes before serving.
Serve with toppings.
8 SERVINGS

Nutrition Information: ⅛ of recipe

Calories 285, Total Fat 9g, Saturated Fat 1g, Cholesterol 0mg,

Sodium 150mg, Dietary Fiber 2g

Serving Tip

When cutting ice cream pies, let pie stand
at room temperature 10 to 15 minutes
before serving. Use a thin, sharp knife.
Between each cut, dip knife in hot water
and wipe dry with paper towel.

There's no guesswork with this easy pie crust, and the end result tastes just like an oatmeal cookie!

CRUST

1	cup QUAKER Oats (quick or old fashioned, uncooked)
¾	cup all-purpose flour
½	cup (1 stick) margarine or butter, melted
¼	cup firmly packed brown sugar

FILLING

Two	21-ounce cans apple or peach pie filling
½	cup raisins
½	teaspoon ground cinnamon

TOPPING

⅓	cup QUAKER Oats (quick or old fashioned, uncooked)
¼	cup all-purpose flour
¼	cup firmly packed brown sugar
3	tablespoons margarine or butter, chilled
	Whipped cream, ice cream or frozen yogurt (optional)

Heat oven to 375°F. Lightly grease 9-inch pie plate. For crust, combine all ingredients; mix well. Press mixture evenly onto bottom and sides of prepared pie plate. Bake 12 to 15 minutes or until golden brown. Cool slightly. For filling, combine all ingredients; pour into prepared crust. For topping, combine dry ingredients; mix well. Cut in margarine until mixture is crumbly; sprinkle evenly over filling. Bake 25 to 30 minutes or until topping is golden brown. Serve topped with whipped cream, ice cream or frozen yogurt, if desired. 8 SERVINGS

Nutrition Information: ⅛ of recipe
Calories 480, Fat 17g, Sodium 250mg, Dietary Fiber 4g

Technique — Whipping Cream

To make sweetened whipped cream, chill small deep bowl and beaters in freezer. Add 1 cup (½ pint) chilled whipping cream and beat on high speed until cream begins to thicken. Add 2 tablespoons powdered sugar and ½ teaspoon vanilla; continue beating just until soft peaks form. Overbeating will turn cream into butter.
Yield: 2 cups whipped cream.

All-Time Holiday Favorites

Holidays, both big and small, give us reason to bake something special — and delicious — for those we love. Here are our favorites.

Hidden inside each scrumptious cookie is a candy surprise.

COOKIES

1	cup (2 sticks) margarine or butter, softened
¾	cup powdered sugar
1	egg
1	teaspoon vanilla
2	cups all-purpose flour
1¼	cups QUAKER Oats (quick or old fashioned, uncooked)
¼	teaspoon salt (optional)

FILLINGS

Approximately 48 assorted bite-size candies such as chocolate, candy-coated chocolate pieces, jelly beans or gumdrops

DECORATIONS

Colored sugar, nonpareils or sprinkles
Powdered sugar*

Heat oven to 325°F. Beat together margarine and sugar until creamy. Add egg and vanilla; beat well. Add combined flour, oats and salt; mix well. Shape dough into 1-inch balls. Press desired candy piece into center of each ball; shape dough around candy so it is completely hidden. Roll cookies in desired decorations until evenly coated. Or, coat in powdered sugar as directed below. Place on ungreased cookie sheet. Bake 14 to 17 minutes or until cookies are set or bottoms are light golden brown. Remove to wire rack. Cool completely. Store in tightly covered container.
ABOUT 4 DOZEN

For powdered sugar cookies: Bake filled cookies as directed above. Remove to wire rack; cool 5 minutes. Place ¾ cup powdered sugar in plastic bag. Add 3 to 4 cookies at a time; shake gently until coated. Sift remaining sugar over cookies.

Nutrition Information: 1 filled cookie
Calories 75, Fat 4g, Sodium 45mg

For Gift-Giving

Pack Holiday Cookie Surprises in tissue-lined holiday tins, or make cookie bundles.
Arrange a few cookies in the center of a square of food-safe tissue, form into a bundle
and tie at the top with a ribbon.

*If you have time to bake only one cookie this holiday season,
make it a memorable one–for Santa and your child.*

½ cup (1 stick) margarine or butter,
  softened
⅔ cup firmly packed brown sugar
¼ cup granulated sugar
1 egg
2 tablespoons milk
1 teaspoon almond extract
¾ cup all-purpose flour
½ teaspoon baking soda
2½ cups QUAKER Oats (quick or
  old fashioned, uncooked)
1 cup dried cherries
1 cup coarsely chopped almonds
  (optional)
  Decorator's icing

Heat oven to 350°F.* Lightly grease two cookie
sheets. Beat together margarine and sugars
until creamy. Add egg, milk and almond
extract; beat well. Add combined flour and
baking soda; mix well. Stir in oats, cherries and
almonds; mix well. Divide dough into 4 equal
portions. With moistened hands, pat dough
onto cookie sheets into ¼-inch-thick holiday
shapes such as stockings or candy canes. Bake
12 to 14 minutes or until edges are light golden
brown. Cool 2 minutes on cookie sheet;
carefully remove to wire rack. Cool completely.
Decorate as desired. Store tightly covered.
4 JUMBO COOKIES

* *For drop cookies:* Drop dough by rounded tablespoonfuls
onto ungreased cookie sheet. Bake at 375°F 10 to 12
minutes or until light golden brown. Cool 1 minute on
cookie sheet; remove to wire rack.
ABOUT 3 DOZEN

Nutrition Information: 1 drop cookie
Calories 90, Fat 3g, Sodium 50mg

Baking with Kids

• Schedule baking for early in the day when everyone is well-rested.

• Dress kids in comfortable, washable clothes.

• Read through recipe together, and give each child a task that's appropriate for his or her age.

• Sit preschoolers at a child-size table, and put decorations in non-breakable bowls. A plastic mat placed beneath the table will simplify cleanup.

Bake It Better Tip

Younger children will have an easier time shaping Santa's Stockings if you lightly grease and flour the cookie sheet. Using your finger, trace the outline of a large stocking. The kids can then spread the dough inside the lines.

CINNAMON OAT ROLLS ♥

Santa and his elves are sure to approve of these orange-glazed cinnamon buns.
Frozen bread dough is a real time-saver.

1 **pound frozen bread dough, thawed completely**
1 **cup QUAKER Oats (quick or old fashioned, uncooked)**
⅓ **cup firmly packed brown sugar**
2 **teaspoons ground cinnamon**
⅓ **cup (5 tablespoons plus 1 teaspoon) margarine or butter, melted**
1 **cup raisins or dried cranberries**
¼ **cup orange marmalade**

Let dough stand, covered, at room temperature 15 minutes to relax. Lightly grease 8- or 9-inch square baking pan. Combine oats, sugar and cinnamon. Add margarine; mix well. Stir in raisins; set aside. Roll dough into 12x10-inch rectangle. (Dough will be very elastic.) Spread evenly with oat mixture to within ½ inch of edges. Roll up, starting from long side,

pinching seam to seal. Cut into 9 slices about 1¼ inches wide; place in prepared pan, cut sides down. Cover loosely with plastic wrap; let rise in warm place 30 minutes or until nearly double in size.

Heat oven to 350°F. Bake uncovered 30 to 35 minutes or until golden brown. Remove from pan; spread tops with marmalade. Serve warm.
9 SERVINGS

To reheat rolls: Wrap in foil. Heat at 350°F 12 to 15 minutes or until warm. Or, unwrap and microwave at HIGH 15 to 20 seconds per roll.

Nutrition Information: 1 roll

Calories 325, Total Fat 9g, Saturated Fat 1g, Cholesterol 0mg

Sodium 375mg, Dietary Fiber 2g

Make It Fun — Packaging Ideas

The whole family can help with packaging homemade cookies and breads for gift-giving. Try these simple ideas.

For Cookies . . .
• Use crayons, felt-tip pens, stickers and stars to decorate plain white paper plates. Place plastic wrap on plates and arrange cookies on top. Wrap with cellophane and tie with ribbon.

• Cover the top and sides of a Quaker oats tube with gift wrap. Line inside of tube with food-safe tissue and fill with cookies.

• Line small red and green gift bags or plastic sand pails with tissue; fill resealable plastic bags with cookies and place in bags or pails. Tie a cookie cutter to the handle with a ribbon.

For Breads . . .
• Place bread on cutting board or tray. Wrap with cellophane and tie with red and green ribbons.

• Arrange muffins in napkin-lined basket. Wrap with cellophane and top with a bow.

64

You'll get professional results with hot roll mix even if you've never baked a yeast bread before.

One 16-ounce can whole berry cranberry sauce
One 16-ounce package hot roll mix
1 cup QUAKER Oats (quick or old fashioned, uncooked)
¼ cup sugar
1 cup hot water (120°F to 130°F)
¼ cup egg substitute or 1 egg, lightly beaten
3 tablespoons margarine or butter, softened
½ cup chopped nuts, divided
2 tablespoons sugar, divided
¾ cup powdered sugar
3 to 4 teaspoons milk
¼ teaspoon vanilla

Lightly grease two cookie sheets. Place cranberry sauce in fine strainer or sieve; stir to break up. Drain; set aside. In large bowl, combine hot roll mix, yeast packet from roll mix, oats and ¼ cup sugar; mix well. Stir in hot water, egg substitute and margarine until dough pulls away from sides of bowl. Knead on lightly floured surface 5 minutes or until smooth and elastic. Divide dough in half. On cookie sheets, pat each half into 12x8-inch rectangle. Top each with half of drained cranberry sauce, ¼ cup nuts and 1 tablespoon sugar spreading to within 1 inch of edges. Roll up, starting from long side; pinch seams and ends to seal. Bring ends together to form a ring. With kitchen shears, cut through ring almost to center at 2-inch intervals. Cover loosely with plastic wrap; let rise in warm place 30 minutes or until nearly double in size.

Heat oven to 350°F. Bake 23 to 28 minutes or until golden brown. Carefully remove to wire rack; cool slightly. For icing, combine remaining ingredients until smooth. Spread over top.
2 COFFEE CAKES

Nutrition Information: ⅛ of coffee cake
Calories 240, Total Fat 6g, Saturated Fat 1g, Cholesterol 0mg, Sodium 220mg, Dietary Fiber 1g

Bake It Better Tip

To decorate wreath, drizzle with icing as recipe directs. While icing is still soft, add pecan halves and whole fresh cranberries; halved red and green candied cherries; or dried cranberries and tiny mint leaves. Or, lightly sprinkle with red and green sugar crystals.

This gingerbread recipe is actually a rolled oatmeal cookie with just enough molasses and spice to appeal to a child's taste.

1 **cup (2 sticks) margarine or butter, softened**
¾ **cup firmly packed brown sugar**
½ **cup molasses**
1 **egg**
3⅓ **cups all-purpose flour**
1½ **cups QUAKER Oats (quick or old fashioned, uncooked)**
1 **teaspoon ground cinnamon**
1 **teaspoon ground ginger**
½ **teaspoon ground nutmeg**
½ **teaspoon baking soda**
¼ **teaspoon salt (optional)**
 Ready prepared frosting or decorator's icing
 Assorted small candies

Beat together margarine and sugar until creamy. Add molasses and egg; beat well. Add combined flour, oats, spices, baking soda and salt; mix well. Divide dough into 2 portions for easier handling. Cover; chill 2 hours.

Heat oven to 350°F. Roll out dough to ¼-inch thickness on lightly floured surface. Cut with 5-inch gingerbread cookie cutter. Bake on ungreased cookie sheet 8 to 10 minutes or until cookies are set. Cool 1 minute on cookie sheet; remove to wire rack. Cool completely. Decorate cookies as desired. Store in tightly covered container.
ABOUT TWENTY 5-INCH COOKIES

Nutrition Information: 1 undecorated cookie
Calories 240, Fat 10g, Sodium 130mg

See photo page 58.

Bake It Better Tip

To make cookies into hanging ornaments, or to use as gift tags, poke hole near top of cookie with drinking straw before baking. Repeat immediately after baking if hole closes.

SWEETHEART COOKIE PUZZLE

A crisp and buttery shortbread-like cookie that's decorated and cut into puzzle-size pieces before baking.

1 **cup (2 sticks) margarine or butter, softened**
½ **cup sugar**
1 **teaspoon vanilla**
2 **cups QUAKER Oats (quick or old fashioned, uncooked)**
1¼ **cups all-purpose flour**
Assorted small candies

Heat oven to 350°F. Lightly grease 2 cookie sheets. Beat together margarine, sugar and vanilla until creamy. Add combined oats and flour; mix well. Divide dough in half. Pat each half into heart shape about ¼ inch thick on prepared cookie sheets. To decorate, gently press candy pieces into dough. With sharp knife, cut through dough to form 8 to 10 random shapes. (Do not separate.) Bake 18 to 20 minutes or until lightly browned. Carefully cut through pieces again to separate. Cool 5 minutes on cookie sheet. Remove to wire rack; cool completely. Store in tightly covered container.

TWO 10-INCH HEARTS

Nutrition Information: 2 undecorated pieces
(based on 8 pieces/heart)
Calories 210, Fat 12g, Sodium 140mg

Bake It Better Tip

To package cookie for gift-giving, line a flat, sturdy cardboard gift box with red or white food-safe tissue. Decorate box top with gift wrap, markers or stickers. Carefully arrange "puzzle pieces" in bottom half of box and close with lid.

Here's a dessert that's perfect for Valentine's Day and pretty enough for any special occasion.

TOPPING

- 2 **cups fresh or frozen peeled, sliced peaches, thawed**
- 2 **cups fresh or frozen raspberries or other berries, thawed**
- 2 **to 3 tablespoons sugar**
- 1 **tablespoon lemon juice**
  Vanilla low-fat yogurt (optional)

SHORTCAKES

- 1½ **cups all-purpose flour**
- 1 **cup QUAKER Oats (quick or old fashioned, uncooked)**
- 3 **tablespoons sugar**
- 1 **tablespoon baking powder**
- ¼ **teaspoon salt (optional)**
- ½ **cup (1 stick) margarine or butter, chilled**
- ⅔ **cup milk**

For topping, combine all ingredients except yogurt; mix gently. Let stand 1 hour.

Heat oven to 425°F. Lightly grease cookie sheet. Combine flour, oats, sugar, baking powder and salt. Cut in margarine with pastry blender or two knives until mixture resembles coarse crumbs. Add milk; mix with fork just until dry ingredients are moistened. Turn out onto lightly floured surface. Knead gently 6 to 8 times. Roll or pat dough ½ inch thick; cut with 2½-inch heart-shaped or round biscuit cutter. Gather dough scraps together (do not knead); reroll and cut until all dough is used. Place on prepared cookie sheet. Bake 12 to 14 minutes or until light golden brown. Remove to wire rack; cool. To serve, split each shortcake in half; top with fruit mixture and, if desired, yogurt.

12 SERVINGS

Nutrition Information: ¹⁄₁₂ of recipe

Calories 210, Fat 9g, Sodium 200mg, Dietary Fiber 2g

Variations

- Substitute raspberry low-fat yogurt for vanilla yogurt.

- Top with lightly sweetened whipped cream instead of yogurt, and substitute sliced fresh strawberries for peaches and raspberries.

- Substitute fresh or frozen blueberries for peaches.

- Sprinkle tops of biscuit hearts with cinnamon-sugar before baking.

*Add these cookie chicks, bunnies and eggs to your child's
Easter basket and watch the smiles.*

1 **cup (2 sticks) margarine or butter,
   softened**
1 **cup sugar**
1 **egg**
2 **tablespoons milk**
1 **teaspoon vanilla**
2½ **cups all-purpose flour**
1 **cup QUAKER Oats (quick or
   old fashioned, uncooked)**
1 **teaspoon baking soda**
½ **teaspoon salt (optional)
   Assorted small candies or
   colored sugar
   Egg Glaze***

Beat together margarine and sugar until
creamy. Add egg, milk and vanilla; beat well.
Add combined flour, oats, baking soda and salt;
mix well. Divide dough into 2 portions for
easier handling. Cover; chill 2 to 3 hours.

Heat oven to 350°F. Roll out dough to ⅛-inch
thickness on lightly floured surface. Cut with
floured assorted 2- to 3-inch cookie cutters.
Place on ungreased cookie sheet. Decorate as
desired. Bake 8 to 10 minutes or until edges
are light golden brown. Cool 1 minute on
cookie sheet; remove to wire rack. Cool
completely. Store in tightly covered container.
ABOUT 4 DOZEN

*For Egg Glaze: Combine 1 egg yolk and ¼ teaspoon
water; divide into 3 small dishes. Tint with food coloring.
With small brush, paint glaze on cookies as desired. Bake
as directed above.

Nutrition Information: 1 undecorated cookie
Calories 80, Fat 4g, Sodium 60mg

Perfect Cut-Out Cookies

• Divide dough into two or three portions
before chilling. Roll one portion at a
time, keeping remainder covered and
chilled.

• With lightly floured rolling pin, roll out
dough on lightly floured surface to an
even thickness; start from center and roll
to edges.

• Using cookie cutters, cut out shapes as
close together as possible. Simple shapes
with sharp edges give the best results.

• Use pancake turner or wide spatula to
transfer cookies to cookie sheet.

• Chill dough scraps before rerolling.

CITRUS STREUSEL SQUARES

Adults will find the sweet-tart filling and crunchy crust of these layered bars appealing.

CRUST AND STREUSEL
- **1 cup (2 sticks) margarine or butter, softened**
- **1½ cups firmly packed brown sugar**
- **2½ cups all-purpose flour**
- **2 cups QUAKER Oats (quick or old fashioned, uncooked)**
- **2 teaspoons baking powder**
- **1 teaspoon salt (optional)**

FILLING
- **One 14-ounce can sweetened condensed milk (not evaporated milk)**
- **¼ cup lemon juice**
- **¼ cup orange juice**
- **2 teaspoons grated lemon peel**
- **2 teaspoons grated orange peel**
  Powdered sugar

Heat oven to 350°F. For crust, beat together margarine and sugar until creamy. Add combined flour, oats, baking powder and salt; mix until crumbly. Reserve 2 cups oat mixture for streusel; set aside. Press remaining oat mixture onto bottom of ungreased 13x9-inch baking pan.

For filling, combine condensed milk, lemon juice, orange juice and peels; mix well. Spread mixture evenly over crust. Sprinkle with reserved oat mixture, patting gently. Bake 35 to 40 minutes or until light golden brown; cool completely. Sprinkle with powdered sugar. Cut into squares. Store tightly covered.
ABOUT 2½ DOZEN

Nutrition Information: 1 bar
Calories 200, Fat 8g, Sodium 120mg

See photo page 70.

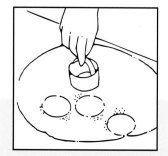

Perfect Biscuits

- Be sure fat is cold; cut into dry ingredients until mixture resembles coarse crumbs.

- Add milk all at once, and stir just until a soft dough forms.

- Knead dough on lightly floured surface quickly and gently, about 6 to 8 times, just until no longer sticky.

- Use floured biscuit cutter and a straight downward motion to cut biscuits. Don't twist the cutter or biscuits may rise unevenly.

- Gather dough scraps; pat to even thickness and cut.

HOT CROSS BISCUITS

Because they use baking powder instead of yeast, Hot Cross Biscuits are much quicker and easier to make than the traditional Easter buns.

1¾ cups all-purpose flour
1   cup QUAKER Oats (quick or old fashioned, uncooked)
2   tablespoons firmly packed brown sugar
2   teaspoons baking powder
1   teaspoon pumpkin pie spice
¼   teaspoon baking soda
¼   teaspoon salt (optional)
⅓   cup (5 tablespoons plus 1 teaspoon) margarine or butter, chilled
¼   cup currants or raisins
1   teaspoon grated orange peel
¾   cup buttermilk
1   tablespoon margarine or butter, melted
⅓   cup powdered sugar
1   to 2 teaspoons milk

Heat oven to 450°F. Lightly grease cookie sheet. Combine first seven ingredients; mix well. Cut in ⅓ cup margarine with pastry blender or two knives until mixture resembles coarse crumbs. Stir in currants and peel. Add buttermilk; mix with fork just until dry ingredients are moistened. Turn out onto lightly floured surface; knead gently 6 to 8 times. Pat dough ½ inch thick. Cut with floured 2½-inch biscuit cutter. Place on prepared cookie sheet. Brush tops with margarine; sprinkle with additional oats, if desired. Bake 10 to 12 minutes or until light golden brown. Remove to wire rack; cool 5 minutes. For icing, mix together powdered sugar and buttermilk; drizzle in a cross shape over each biscuit.

1 DOZEN

Nutrition Information: 1 biscuit
Calories 190, Fat 7g, Sodium 220mg, Dietary Fiber 1g

*For a star-spangled finale, a crisp oat shortbread crust is topped with
a cool and creamy cheesecake filling and fresh berries.*

CRUST

1	cup QUAKER Oats (quick or old fashioned, uncooked)
¾	cup all-purpose flour
⅓	cup firmly packed brown sugar
¼	cup chopped nuts (optional)
¼	teaspoon baking soda
¼	teaspoon salt (optional)
⅓	cup (5 tablespoons plus 1 teaspoon) margarine or butter, melted

FILLING

Two	8-ounce packages cream cheese, softened
¾	cup granulated sugar
2	tablespoons all-purpose flour
2	eggs
1	teaspoon vanilla

FRUIT TOPPING

2	cups blueberries, raspberries or sliced strawberries
½	cup strawberry preserves

Heat oven to 350°F. Lightly grease 13x9-inch baking pan. For crust, combine oats, flour, sugar, nuts, baking soda and salt; mix well. Add margarine; mix until crumbly. Press oat mixture onto bottom of prepared pan. Bake 10 minutes.

For filling, beat together cream cheese, sugar and flour until creamy. Add eggs and vanilla; beat well. Pour over crust, spreading evenly. Bake 25 minutes or until set. Cool completely; chill.

For topping, combine blueberries and preserves. To serve, cut into bars; top with fruit. Store tightly covered in refrigerator.

24 BARS

Nutrition Information: 1 fruit-topped bar
Calories 180, Fat 10g, Sodium 100mg

Picnic Pointer

If bars will be carried to picnic site, pack bars and fruit topping in separate sealed containers in cooler with cold packs. Just before serving, cut bars, and top with fruit. Keep leftovers cold.

Treat Halloween goblins to a big oatmeal cookie on a stick. They're easy to make and lots of fun to decorate.

1 **cup (2 sticks) margarine or butter, softened**
1¼ **cups firmly packed brown sugar**
2 **eggs**
2 **tablespoons milk**
2½ **cups QUAKER Oats (quick or old fashioned, uncooked)**
2 **cups all-purpose flour**
2 **teaspoons baking powder**
1 **teaspoon ground cinnamon**
¼ **teaspoon baking soda**
¼ **teaspoon salt (optional)**
Flat wooden sticks
Ready prepared frosting
Assorted small candy pieces

Beat together margarine and sugar until creamy. Add eggs and milk; beat well. Add combined oats, flour, baking powder, cinnamon, baking soda and salt; mix well. Cover; chill about 2 hours.

Heat oven to 375°F. Shape dough into 1½-inch balls. Place 3 inches apart on ungreased cookie sheet. Insert wooden stick into side of each ball. Using bottom of glass dipped in granulated sugar, flatten to 2½-inch diameter. Bake 14 to 16 minutes or until edges are light golden brown. Cool 1 minute on cookie sheet; remove to wire rack. Cool completely. Decorate as desired. Store in tightly covered container. ABOUT 2½ DOZEN

Nutrition Information: 1 undecorated cookie
Calories 150, Fat 7g, Sodium 110mg

Bake It Better Tip

Flat wooden sticks can be found in stores that sell craft supplies. If cookie pops will be used as party favors, wrap each cookie with clear plastic wrap and tie closed with ribbon.

FROSTED PUMPKIN SOFTIES

A simple cream cheese frosting complements these cake-like cookies.

COOKIES

1	cup (2 sticks) margarine or butter, softened
¾	cup firmly packed brown sugar
¾	cup granulated sugar
1	cup canned pumpkin
1	egg
1	teaspoon vanilla
2½	cups QUAKER Oats (quick or old fashioned, uncooked)
1¾	cups all-purpose flour
1	teaspoon pumpkin pie spice or ground cinnamon
1	teaspoon baking soda
¼	teaspoon salt (optional)

FROSTING

One	3-ounce package cream cheese, softened
1	tablespoon milk
½	teaspoon vanilla
2½	cups powdered sugar
	Yellow and red food coloring

Heat oven to 350°F. Beat together margarine and sugars until creamy. Add pumpkin, egg and vanilla; beat well. Add combined oats, flour, pumpkin pie spice, baking soda and salt; mix well. Drop by rounded tablespoonfuls onto ungreased cookie sheet. Bake 11 to 13 minutes or until light golden brown. Cool 1 minute on cookie sheet; remove to wire rack. Cool completely.

For frosting, beat together cream cheese, milk and vanilla until smooth. Gradually beat in powdered sugar until smooth; tint with food coloring, if desired. Frost top of each cookie. Store in tightly covered container in refrigerator.

ABOUT 4 DOZEN

Nutrition Information: 1 frosted cookie
Calories 130, Fat 5g, Sodium 70mg

Bake It Better Tip

Bright, shiny cookie sheets prevent cookies from becoming too brown on the bottoms. Cookie sheets without rims help cookies brown more evenly.

Expect requests for seconds and bake an extra. It's that easy—and delicious.

CRUST

- 1 cup QUAKER Oats (quick or old fashioned, uncooked)
- ¾ cup all-purpose flour
- ½ cup (1 stick) margarine or butter, melted
- ¼ cup firmly packed brown sugar

FILLING

- Two 8-ounce packages cream cheese, softened*
- One 16-ounce can (1¾ cups) pumpkin
- 1½ cups powdered sugar
- 2 teaspoons vanilla
- 2 teaspoons ground cinnamon
- ½ teaspoon ground nutmeg
- ½ teaspoon ground ginger
- 2 cups thawed nondairy whipped topping
- ¼ cup coarsely chopped pecans (optional)

Heat oven to 375°F. Lightly grease 9-inch pie plate. For crust, combine all ingredients; mix well. Press mixture evenly onto bottom and sides of prepared pie plate. Bake 12 to 15 minutes or until golden brown. Cool completely.

For filling, in large mixing bowl, combine first seven ingredients. Beat on medium speed of electric mixer until smooth, about 1 to 2 minutes. By hand, gently fold in whipped topping. Spread filling into prepared crust. Top with pecans, if desired. Chill at least 3 hours or overnight.

10 SERVINGS

To soften cream cheese: Place in large microwaveable bowl. Microwave at HIGH 30 seconds or until softened.

Nutrition Information: ¹⁄₁₀ of recipe
Calories 470, Fat 30g, Sodium 250mg

Pumpkin Pointers

- Be sure to purchase canned pumpkin, not pumpkin pie filling, for these recipes.

- Leftover canned pumpkin can be stored in the refrigerator up to a week or frozen. To freeze, transfer to freezer-safe container, label and freeze up to six months. Thaw in refrigerator before using.

- To make your own pumpkin pie spice, combine 4 teaspoons cinnamon, 1 teaspoon ginger, ½ teaspoon allspice, ½ teaspoon cloves and ½ teaspoon nutmeg in small container with tight-fitting lid. Store in cool, dark cabinet.

Just for Kids

An afternoon of baking offers immeasurable rewards for everyone. And, it's an activity that requires no more planning than a trip to the grocery store. Why not bake some memories today?

From itty-bitty, to big as a pizza, all you need is one great cookie dough, and this is it.

1   **cup (2 sticks) margarine or butter, softened**
1¼ **cups firmly packed brown sugar**
½   **cup granulated sugar**
2   **eggs**
2   **tablespoons milk**
2   **teaspoons vanilla**
1¾ **cups all-purpose flour**
1   **teaspoon baking soda**
½   **teaspoon salt (optional)**
2½ **cups QUAKER Oats (quick or old fashioned, uncooked)**
2   **cups (12 ounces) semisweet chocolate pieces**
1   **cup coarsely chopped nuts (optional)**

Determine desired cookie size; heat oven to temperature directed. Beat margarine and sugars until creamy. Add eggs, milk and vanilla; beat well. Add combined flour, baking soda and salt. Stir in oats, chocolate pieces and nuts; mix well. Portion dough into desired size; bake as directed. Cool 1 minute on cookie sheet; remove to wire rack. Cool completely.

Mini Cookies:
Heat oven to 375°F. Drop by rounded teaspoonfuls onto ungreased cookie sheet. Bake 9 to 10 minutes or until light golden brown.
ABOUT 8 DOZEN
Nutrition Information: 1 cookie
Calories 65, Fat 3g, Sodium 40mg

In-the-Middle Cookies:
Heat oven to 375°F. Drop by rounded tablespoonfuls onto ungreased cookie sheet. Bake 9 to 10 minutes for chewy cookies or 12 to 13 minutes for crisp cookies.
ABOUT 5 DOZEN
Nutrition Information: 1 cookie
Calories 110, Fat 5g, Sodium 60mg

Big Tips for Big Cookies

• To prevent dough from sticking to fingers when shaping the *monster*, dip fingers into granulated sugar.

• Test cookies after the *minimum* baking time. When baking chewy cookies, your finger should leave a slight impression in the center.

• Let *megas* and *monsters* cool a few minutes on cookie sheets before transferring to cooling rack. Use two large, wide spatulas or pancake turners to transfer the *monster*.

• To serve the *monster*, place cookie on cutting board. Use a sharp knife to cut into wedges, pizza-style.

Mega Cookies:

Heat oven to 350°F. Drop by ¼ measuring cupfuls about 4 inches apart onto ungreased cookie sheets. Bake 17 to 19 minutes for chewy cookies or 20 to 22 minutes for crisp cookies.
ABOUT 2 DOZEN

Monster Cookies:

Heat oven to 350°F. Lightly grease 2 large cookie sheets. Divide dough in half. Spread each half to 11-inch diameter on prepared cookie sheet. Bake 25 to 30 minutes for chewy cookies or 30 to 35 minutes for crisp cookies. Cut each cookie into 12 wedges while still warm.
2 DOZEN

Nutrition Information:

Mega Cookies (1 cookie) or *Monster Cookies* (¹⁄₁₂ of cookie):
Calories 270, Fat 13g, Sodium 150mg

VARIATIONS:
Signature Oatmeal Cookies

Prepare cookies as recipe directs except substitute 1 cup (any combination of) raisins, diced dried mixed fruit, crushed toffee pieces or candy-coated chocolate pieces for 1 cup semisweet chocolate pieces.

Ice Cream Sandwich Cookies

Spread softened ice cream or frozen yogurt on bottom side of one cookie; top with second cookie. If desired, roll edges in nonpareils, sprinkles or mini semisweet chocolate pieces. Wrap in plastic wrap or aluminum foil; freeze. Remove from freezer a few minutes before serving.

Fun-Filled Sandwich Cookies

Spread ready prepared frosting or marshmallow creme on bottom side of one cookie; top with second cookie.

Peanut Butter Sandwich Cookies

Beat together ¾ cup peanut butter, ¼ cup margarine or butter, 1½ cups powdered sugar and 3 tablespoons milk until smooth. (Mixture will be stiff.) Spread on bottom side of one cookie; top with second cookie.

Oatmeal Cookie Sandwich Pops

Insert flat wooden stick into filling of any sandwich cookie.

Measuring How-Tos

• Spoon dry ingredients into nested dry measuring cups (plastic or metal) and level with a metal spatula.

• Measure liquid ingredients in a glass or plastic measure with a spout for pouring. For accuracy, place cup on level surface, pour in liquid and read measure at eye level.

• Thick or sticky ingredients like peanut butter and shortening also should be measured in nested dry measuring cups. Press firmly into cup to eliminate air bubbles and level even with top of cup.

NO-BAKE OAT TREATS

Older kids with some experience in the kitchen can make these candy-like peanut butter oatmeal cookies on their own.

1 cup peanut butter
1 cup powdered sugar
½ cup milk
1 teaspoon vanilla
2 cups QUAKER Oats (quick or old fashioned, uncooked)
2 cups (any combination of) raisins, diced dried mixed fruit, miniature marshmallows, flaked coconut, chopped peanuts or semisweet chocolate pieces

Mix together first four ingredients. Stir in oats and remaining ingredients. Drop by rounded teaspoonfuls onto waxed paper. Store in tightly covered container.
ABOUT 4 DOZEN

Nutrition Information: 1 piece
Calories 75, Fat 3g, Sodium 25mg

APPLESAUCE RAISIN CHEWS

These are the perfect back-to-school cookies—soft and chewy, quick and easy and sturdy enough to pack in a lunch bag.

1 cup (2 sticks) margarine or butter, softened
1 cup firmly packed brown sugar
1 cup applesauce
1 egg
1 teaspoon vanilla
2 cups all-purpose flour
1 teaspoon baking soda
1 teaspoon ground cinnamon
½ teaspoon salt (optional)
2½ cups QUAKER Oats (quick or old fashioned, uncooked)
1 cup raisins

Heat oven to 350°F. Beat together margarine and sugar until creamy. Add applesauce, egg and vanilla; beat well. Add combined flour, baking soda, cinnamon and salt; mix well. Stir in oats and raisins. Drop by rounded tablespoonfuls onto ungreased cookie sheet. Bake 11 to 13 minutes or until light golden brown. Cool 1 minute on cookie sheet; remove to wire rack. Cool completely. Store in tightly covered container.
ABOUT 4 DOZEN

Nutrition Information: 1 cookie
Calories 100, Fat 4g, Sodium 65mg

Here's a cookie with kid-pleasing flavors that's perfect for summer.

1 **cup (6 ounces) semisweet chocolate pieces**
⅓ **cup (5 tablespoons plus 1 teaspoon) margarine or butter**
16 **large marshmallows**
1 **teaspoon vanilla**
2 **cups QUAKER Oats (quick or old fashioned, uncooked)**
1 **cup (any combination of) raisins, diced dried mixed fruit, flaked coconut, miniature marshmallows or chopped nuts**

In large saucepan over low heat, melt chocolate pieces, margarine and marshmallows, stirring until smooth. Remove from heat; cool slightly. Stir in remaining ingredients. Drop by rounded teaspoonfuls onto waxed paper. Chill 2 to 3 hours. Let stand at room temperature about 15 minutes before serving. Store in tightly covered container in refrigerator.
3 DOZEN

MICROWAVE DIRECTIONS: Place chocolate pieces, margarine and marshmallows in large microwaveable bowl. Microwave at HIGH 1 to 2 minutes or until mixture is melted and smooth, stirring every 30 seconds. Proceed as recipe directs.

Nutrition Information: 1 piece
Calories 75, Fat 3g, Sodium 20mg

See photo page 84.

Using The Microwave Safely

• Children who are under the age of seven or who are unfamiliar with microwave cooking should have adult supervision.

• Be sure the microwave oven can be reached easily by your child and that the control panel is easy to see.

• Microwave cookware that's lightweight, unbreakable and equipped with handles is safest for kids. Mark cookware that's okay for your kids to use with a permanent marker.

• During cooking, stir food or rotate container a half-turn to distribute heat and prevent hot spots.

• Teach kids to use potholders to remove containers from the microwave oven and to uncover hot containers away from their face.

*There's plenty of room for frosting, decorations and a birthday message.
And don't forget the candles!*

½ **cup (1 stick) margarine or butter, softened**
½ **cup sugar**
 1 **egg**
 1 **teaspoon vanilla**
 1 **cup all-purpose flour**
 1 **cup QUAKER Oats (quick or old fashioned, uncooked)**
¼ **teaspoon baking soda**
¼ **teaspoon salt (optional)**
    Ready prepared frosting
    Assorted small candy pieces

Heat oven to 350°F. Lightly grease 1 large cookie sheet. Beat margarine and sugar until creamy. Add egg and vanilla; beat well. Add combined flour, oats, baking soda and salt; mix well. Spread dough onto prepared cookie sheet to 10-inch diameter, about ½ inch thick. Bake 22 to 25 minutes or until light golden brown. Cool 5 minutes on cookie sheet; carefully loosen with spatula. Remove to wire rack; cool completely. To decorate, spread frosting over surface of cookie; gently press candy pieces into frosting. Cut into wedges to serve.

12 SERVINGS

Nutrition Information: ¹⁄₁₂ of undecorated cookie
Calories 170, Fat 9g, Sodium 110mg

Bake It Better Tip

To make cookie look like a pizza, tint prepared vanilla frosting with red and yellow food coloring to resemble pizza sauce. Decorate with flaked coconut (cheese), halved black gumdrops or jelly beans (olives), strawberry or cherry fruit roll-ups cut into circles (pepperoni) and green gummy worms (green pepper strips).

HAPPY BIRTHDAY

BANANA SPLIT SUNDAE COOKIES

Say "happy birthday" to a special someone who's six or 60 with a cookie sundae.

1   cup (2 sticks) margarine or butter, softened
1   cup firmly packed brown sugar
1½   cups mashed ripe banana (about 4 medium)
2   eggs
2   teaspoons vanilla
2½   cups QUAKER Oats (quick or old fashioned, uncooked)
2   cups all-purpose flour
1   teaspoon baking soda
¼   teaspoon salt (optional)
1   cup (6 ounces) semisweet chocolate pieces
     Ice cream or frozen yogurt
     Ice cream topping, any flavor

Heat oven to 350°F. Beat together margarine and sugar until creamy. Add banana, eggs and vanilla; beat well. Add combined oats, flour, baking soda and salt; mix well. Stir in chocolate pieces; mix well. Drop by ¼ measuring cupfuls onto ungreased cookie sheet about 3 inches apart. Spread dough to 3½-inch diameter. Bake 14 to 16 minutes or until edges are light golden brown. Cool 1 minute on cookie sheet; remove to wire rack. Cool completely. To serve, top each cookie with a scoop of ice cream and ice cream topping.
ABOUT 2 DOZEN

Nutrition Information: 1 cookie (without ice cream or topping)
Calories 225, Fat 11g, Sodium 130mg

Party Idea

Create your own sundae bar. Arrange cookies on large platter. Choose several flavors of ice cream and toppings. (Stand cartons of ice cream in large bowl filled with ice.) Use small bowls to hold sliced bananas and strawberries, chopped nuts, chocolate chips and sprinkles.

CHUNKY FRUIT OATMEAL COOKIES

At last, an oatmeal cookie that's chunk-full of fruit and nuts.

¾ cup (1½ sticks) margarine or butter, softened
¾ cup firmly packed brown sugar
½ cup granulated sugar
¼ cup milk
1 egg white or 1 egg
1½ teaspoons vanilla
3 cups QUAKER Oats (quick or old fashioned, uncooked)
1 cup all-purpose flour
½ teaspoon baking soda
½ teaspoon salt (optional)
One 6-ounce package diced dried mixed fruit
1 cup coarsely chopped nuts

Heat oven to 350°F. Lightly grease cookie sheet. Beat together margarine and sugars until creamy. Add milk, egg white and vanilla; beat well. Add combined oats, flour, baking soda and salt; mix well. Stir in dried fruit and nuts. Drop by ¼ measuring cupfuls onto prepared cookie sheet about 3 inches apart. Flatten to 3-inch diameter. Bake 10 to 12 minutes or until golden brown. Cool 1 minute on cookie sheet; remove to wire rack. Cool completely. Store in tightly covered container.
ABOUT 2 DOZEN

Nutrition Information: 1 cookie
Calories 200, Fat 10g, Sodium 90mg

Brown Bag Tip

Freeze cookies in individual sandwich or snack-size resealable bags (2 cookies per bag), or individually wrap them. You'll save time packing lunch boxes, and the cookies will thaw by lunchtime.

These mini muffins will remind you of a chocolate-covered banana.

1¼ cups all-purpose flour
 1 cup QUAKER Oats (quick or
    old fashioned, uncooked)
 ½ cup firmly packed brown sugar
 ⅓ cup unsweetened cocoa powder
 1 tablespoon baking powder
 ¼ teaspoon baking soda
 ⅔ cup mashed ripe banana
    (about 2 medium)
 ½ cup milk
 ⅓ cup (5 tablespoons plus 1 teaspoon)
    margarine or butter, melted
 2 egg whites or 1 egg
 1 teaspoon vanilla
    Powdered sugar (optional)

Heat oven to 400°F. Line 30 miniature muffin cups with paper baking cups, or lightly grease bottoms only.* Combine flour, oats, sugar, cocoa powder, baking powder and baking soda; mix well. Add combined banana, milk, margarine, egg whites and vanilla; mix just until dry ingredients are moistened. Fill muffin cups almost full. Bake 10 to 12 minutes or until wooden pick inserted in center comes out clean. Let muffins stand a few minutes; remove from pan. Cool; sprinkle with powdered sugar.

2½ DOZEN MINIATURE MUFFINS

*Or use 12 medium muffin cups. Bake 20 to 25 minutes or until wooden pick inserted in center comes out clean.

Nutrition Information: 1 miniature muffin
Calories 70, Total Fat 2g, Saturated Fat 0g, Cholesterol 0mg, Sodium 80mg, Dietary Fiber 1g

Bake It Better Tip

Because the capacity of muffin pans varies, some recipes may make less than a dozen muffins. To keep the heat evenly distributed, fill any empty cups with a tablespoon or two of water.

92

Don't wait for a rainy day to bake some fun. These whole grain pretzels taste terrific and are a wholesome snack.

3	to 3½ cups all-purpose flour
1¼	cups QUAKER Oats (quick or old fashioned, uncooked)
2	tablespoons sugar
One	¼-ounce package quick-rising yeast
1½	teaspoons salt
¾	cup milk
¾	cup water
2	tablespoons margarine or butter
1	egg, lightly beaten

In large mixing bowl, combine 2 cups flour, oats, sugar, yeast and salt; mix well. Heat milk, water and margarine until very warm (120°F to 130°F). Add to flour mixture. Blend at low speed of electric mixer until dry ingredients are moistened. Increase to medium speed; beat 3 minutes. By hand, gradually stir in enough remaining flour to make a soft dough that pulls away from sides of bowl. Knead on lightly floured surface 5 minutes or until smooth and elastic, adding additional flour if dough is sticky. Cover loosely with plastic wrap; let dough rest 10 minutes.

Heat oven to 350°F. Lightly grease cookie sheet. Divide dough into 24 equal pieces. Roll each piece between surface and palms of hands into a 12-inch rope. Shape into pretzels, letters or numbers; place on cookie sheet. Cover loosely with plastic wrap; let rest 10 minutes or until slightly risen. Brush tops of pretzels with beaten egg. Sprinkle with additional oats, if desired, patting lightly. Bake 15 to 18 minutes or until golden brown. Remove from cookie sheet; cool on wire rack. Store in tightly covered container. 2 DOZEN

Nutrition Information: 1 pretzel
Calories 110, Total Fat 2g, Saturated Fat 0g, Cholesterol 10mg,
Sodium 160mg, Dietary Fiber 1g

To Shape Pretzels

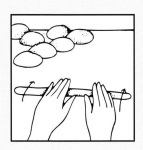

• Divide dough into 24 equal pieces; roll each piece into a 12-inch rope.

• Curve ends of each rope to make a circle; cross ends at top. Twist ends once, and lay over bottom of circle. Brush with beaten egg; sprinkle with oats.

SURPRISE OAT BUNS

The treat hidden in the center of each bun adds an element of surprise.

DOUGH

One **16-ounce package hot roll mix**
- **1 cup QUAKER Oats (quick or old fashioned, uncooked)**
- **¼ cup granulated sugar**
- **1 cup hot water (120°F to 130°F)**
- **1 egg, room temperature, lightly beaten**
- **3 tablespoons margarine or butter, softened**

FILLINGS
- **32 bite-size pieces (any combination of) apple chunks, caramels, chocolate, dried apricots or tablespoon portions of peanut butter**

STREUSEL
- **½ cup QUAKER Oats (quick or old fashioned, uncooked)**
- **½ cup all-purpose flour**
- **⅓ cup firmly packed brown sugar**
- **¼ cup (½ stick) margarine or butter, melted**

Lightly grease 13x9-inch baking pan. In large bowl, combine hot roll mix, yeast packet from roll mix, oats and sugar; mix well. Stir in hot water, egg and margarine; mix until dough pulls away from sides of bowl. Knead on lightly floured surface 5 minutes or until smooth and elastic, adding additional flour if dough is sticky. Divide dough in half. Cover one half with plastic wrap; set aside. Divide remaining half into 16 equal pieces. Shape dough into balls; flatten to ¼-inch thickness. Place filling in center of each circle; pinch edges together to seal in filling. Arrange in single layer in prepared pan. Repeat with remaining dough. Cover loosely with plastic wrap; let dough rise in warm place 30 to 40 minutes or until buns are touching.

Heat oven to 375°F. For streusel, combine dry ingredients. Add margarine; mix well. Sprinkle evenly over tops of buns. Bake 25 to 30 minutes or until light golden brown. Cool 10 minutes; remove buns by inverting pan onto baking sheet. Invert again onto serving platter so that streusel is on top. Serve warm. Store tightly covered.

32 BUNS

Nutrition Information: 1 apple-filled bun
Calories 110, Fat 3g, Sodium 120mg

INDEX

INDEX